**Frommer's®**

KU-070-448

# Paris
## day BY day

### 1st Edition

## by Christi Daugherty

WILEY

Wiley Publishing, Inc.

# Contents

Published by:

## Wiley Publishing, Inc.

111 River St.
Hoboken, NJ 07030-5774

ISBN-13: 978-0-7645-7982-0
ISBN-10: 0-7645-7982-7

Editor: Christine Ryan
*Special thanks to Marc Nadeau*
Production Editor: Suzanna R. Thompson
Photo Editor: Richard Fox
Cartographers: Nicholas Trotter and Andrew Murphy
Production by Wiley Indianapolis Composition Services
Savvy Traveler illustrations by Karl Brandt and Rashell Smith

For information on our other products and services or to obtain technical
support, please contact our Customer Care Department within the U.S.
at 800/762-2974, outside the U.S. at 317/572-3993 or fax 317/572-4002.

Wiley also publishes its books in a variety of electronic formats. Some
content that appears in print may not be available in electronic formats.

Manufactured in China

10 9 8 7

# A Note from the Publisher

Organizing your time. That's what this guide is all about.

Other guides give you long lists of things to see and do and then expect you to fit the pieces together. The Day by Day guides are different. These guides tell you the best of everything, and then they show you how to see it *in the smartest, most time-efficient way.* Our authors have designed detailed itineraries organized by time, neighborhood, or special interest. And each tour comes with a bulleted map that takes you from stop to stop.

Hoping to follow Hemingway's footsteps, or to tour the highlights of the Louvre? Planning a walk through Montmartre, or a whirlwind tour of the very best that Paris has to offer? Whatever your interest or schedule, the Day by Days give you the smartest route to follow. Not only do we take you to the top sights and attractions, but we also introduce you to those special moments that only locals know about—those "finds" that turn tourists into travelers.

The Day by Days are also your top choice if you're looking for one complete guide for all your travel needs. The best hotels and restaurants for every budget, the greatest shopping values, the wildest nightlife—it's all here.

Why should you trust our judgment? Because our authors personally visit each place they write about. They're an independent lot who say what they think and would never include places they wouldn't recommend to their best friends. They're also open to suggestions from readers. If you'd like to contact them, please send your comments my way at mspring@wiley.com, and I'll pass them on.

Enjoy your Day by Day guide—the most helpful travel companion you can buy. And have the trip of a lifetime.

Warm regards,

Michael Spring, Publisher
Frommer's Travel Guides

## About the Author

After working for years as an investigative newspaper reporter, **Christi Daugherty** decided to leave that gritty life behind in 2000 and see the world—or at least Europe. Leaving her long-time home in New Orleans, she moved to England, which she uses as a base for writing and editing travel guidebooks for publishers around the world. Her work has also appeared in the *Dallas Morning News,* the *Washington Post,* and the *Financial Times.* She is currently writing *Frommer's Ireland 2006.*

## Acknowledgments

Special thanks to Jack Jewers and Christopher Moore for their help and enthusiasm.

## An Additional Note

Please be advised that travel information is subject to change at any time—and this is especially true of prices. We therefore suggest that you write or call ahead for confirmation when making your travel plans. The authors, editors, and publisher cannot be held responsible for the experiences of readers while traveling. Your safety is important to us, however, so we encourage you to stay alert and be aware of your surroundings.

## Star Ratings, Icons & Abbreviations

Every hotel, restaurant, and attraction listing in this guide has been ranked for quality, value, service, amenities, and special features using a **star-rating system.** Hotels, restaurants, attractions, shopping, and nightlife are rated on a scale of zero stars (recommended) to three stars (exceptional). In addition to the star-rating system, we also use a **kids icon** to point out the best bets for families. Within each tour, we recommend cafes, bars, or restaurants where you can take a break. Each of these stops appears in a shaded box marked with a coffee cup–shaped bullet .

The following **abbreviations** are used for credit cards:

| AE | American Express | DISC | Discover | V | Visa |
|----|------------------|------|----------|---|------|
| DC | Diners Club | MC | MasterCard | | |

## Frommers.com

Now that you have the guidebook to a great trip, visit our website at **www. frommers.com** for travel information on more than 3,000 destinations. With features updated regularly, we give you instant access to the most current trip-planning information available. At Frommers.com, you'll also find the best prices on airfares, accommodations, and car rentals—and you can even book travel online through our travel booking partners.

## A Note on Prices

Frommer's provides exact prices in each destination's local currency. As this book went to press, the rate of exchange was 1€ = US$1.30. Rates of exchange are constantly in flux; for up-to-the-minute information, consult a currency-conversion website such as www.oanda.com/convert/classic.

In the "Take a Break" and "Best Bets" sections of this book, we have used a system of dollar signs to show a range of costs for 1 night in a hotel (the price of a double-occupancy room) or the cost of an entree at a restaurant. Use the following table to decipher the dollar signs:

| Cost | Hotels | Restaurants |
|------|--------|-------------|
| $ | under $100 | under $10 |
| $$ | $100–$200 | $10–$20 |
| $$$ | $200–$300 | $20–$30 |
| $$$$ | $300–$400 | $30–$40 |
| $$$$$ | over $400 | over $40 |

## An Invitation to the Reader

In researching this book, we discovered many wonderful places—hotels, restaurants, shops, and more. We're sure you'll find others. Please tell us about them, so we can share the information with your fellow travelers in upcoming editions. If you were disappointed with a recommendation, we'd love to know that, too. Please write to:

*Frommer's Paris Day by Day,* 1st Edition
Wiley Publishing, Inc. • 111 River St. • Hoboken, NJ 07030-5774

# 12 Favorite
## Moments

# 12 Favorite **Moments**

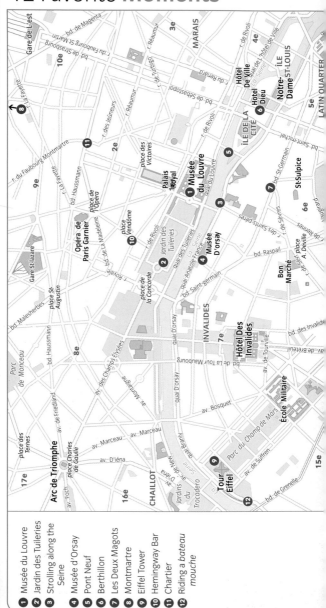

Waiting for the Eiffel Tower to light up after dark, strolling along the Seine on a warm summer night—these are some of my favorite moments in the world, not just in Paris. This is an electric city, a place that sends a charge through you the moment you arrive. Here are a few things I always try to do, see, or feel when I'm here. I hope you like them as much as I do.

**1 Walking through the courtyard of the Musée du Louvre** early in the morning, hurrying to be one of the first in line, and catching the sun glinting off the glass pyramids in the courtyard always gives me a sense of excitement. I feel dwarfed by the looming walls as I wait for the beauty that lies within. *See p 26.*

**2 Wandering through the Jardin des Tuileries** and catching peeks of the Eiffel Tower in the distance as the crowds swirl around me. I always take a photo of a different statue with my cellphone, and use that photo as a screensaver for the next few months—just to remind me. *See p 90.*

**3 Walking along the Seine on a warm summer night** toward the islands, watching the tour boats *(bateaux mouches)* cruise slowly by, the lights from their windows

*Art lovers lining up to get into the Louvre.*

reflecting on the river. The riverside is packed, even after 10pm; sometimes it seems as if everybody in Paris is here. Bands play, lovers kiss, children frolic, everybody smiles—this is how life should be all the time. *See p 136.*

**4 Sitting in the Musée d'Orsay** in the center sculpture court, down below the entrance, looking up at the huge, ornate clock on the wall far above. Through the frosted glass around it you can see the shadows of people passing by on invisible walkways. The sheer scale is astounding; the look is pure drama. And all around me the works of history's most talented sculptors lounge, leap, and laugh silently. *See p 7.*

**5 Walking across the pont Neuf,** passing buskers, artists, teenagers, and jazz bands, and then reaching the Ile de la Cité, where peaceful streets are shaded by the tall buildings. I spend hours in the island's sophisticated boutiques, trying on French scarves and tiny little earrings, and practicing my French on the shop owners. *See p 61.*

**6 Getting an ice cream from Berthillon** on Ile St-Louis. This ice-cream shop is arguably the most famous in Paris, and Parisians love their ice cream, so that's saying something. It's tucked into a quiet street, and always, from the moment it opens until it closes, has a line out front. On bright days, I get a cup of hazelnut and vanilla, then walk down to the riverside to eat it in the sunshine. *See p 63.*

**7 Having wine at Les Deux Magots,** solely because F. Scott Fitzgerald and Ernest Hemingway loved this place. Today, it's too touristy, too expensive, too noisy . . . but I don't care. So much literary history happened here, and the waiters don't mind that much if all you want to do is have a small carafe of red wine, read *This Side of Paradise*, and soak up the ambience. It must have looked almost exactly the same in the 1920s. *See p 39.*

**8 Climbing the streets of Montmartre.** This hilly, hopelessly romantic neighborhood is my favorite in all of Paris. A sweeping view of the city spreads out before you from every cross street. Every corner reveals another evocative stone staircase too steep to see all the way down, but at the bottom you know you'll find sweet old buildings painted pale colors, and streets of old paving stones. On a gray, autumnal day, I want to be here. *See p 68.*

**9 Sitting outside the Eiffel Tower at sunset,** licking an ice-cream cone and waiting for the lights to come on. That moment when somebody, somewhere, flicks the button that lights up the tower, from the bottom to the top, is matchless. Then I know where I am. *See p 25.*

**10 Lingering over a cocktail at the Hemingway Bar** in the Hotel Ritz. The hotel is ultra-luxurious, but the bartenders are relaxed and friendly, and they mix a mean vodka martini. I like to bring a book, sit in the corner, and wonder what it was like when Hemingway and Fitzgerald used to spend far too much time here. *See p 15.*

**11 Enjoying steak frites at Chartier,** where the waiters manage to be both brusque and friendly, and approve of my efforts to speak French. It's an inexpensive yet classically French restaurant. At the end of my meal, the waiters add up the bill on the white paper covering the table. They also smile at my bad French jokes. *See p 108.*

**12 Riding a *bateau mouche*** down the Seine, where all the buildings are artfully lighted so they seem to glow from within. On warm nights, I take an open-top boat, and feel as if I can reach up and touch the damp, stone bridges as we pass beneath them. *See p 11.* ●

*The Eiffel Tower just after sunset.*

# The Best **in One Day**

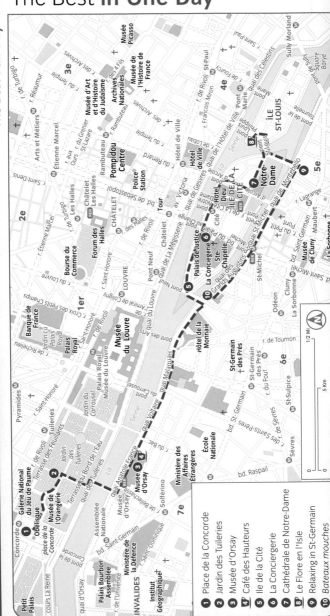

1. Place de la Concorde
2. Jardin des Tuileries
3. Musée d'Orsay
4. Café des Hauteurs
5. Ile de la Cité
6. La Conciergerie
7. Cathédrale de Notre-Dame
8. Le Flore en l'Isle
9. Relaxing in St-Germain
10. Bateaux mouches

This 1-day tour includes everything I would want to see if I had only 24 hours in the City of Light. It's an ambitious itinerary, so start early and wear comfortable shoes. But make sure they're stylish—remember, you're in Paris. START: **Métro to Concorde**

**1 ★★ Place de la Concorde.** This is the city's largest square, and a good place to get immediate Paris gratification. Position yourself so that you can see down the long straight line of the Champs Elysées to the formidable Arc de Triomphe, a monument to Napoleon's conquests. Now turn 180 degrees, and find the sprawling palace that houses the Louvre Museum right in front of you. From here, you'll see the massive 19th-century Madeleine Church to your left. On your right, across the Seine, is the Assemblée Nationale (home to the lower house of the French Parliament). Amid the square's tourists, peddlers, and hustlers stands the sleek Luxor Obelisk (a gift from Egypt), near the spot where, in 1792, a guillotine was built to execute Louis XVI and Marie Antoinette. This perfect, lovely viewpoint is your own instant postcard. Welcome to Paris. ⏱ *10 min.; go early in the morning to avoid crowds, or just after sunset to see the edifices aglow. Free admission. Métro: Concorde.*

**2 Jardin des Tuileries.** Place de la Concorde ends where the Louvre's stately gardens begin. On a space about the size of two football fields, lacy chestnut trees shade sculpted paths that stretch off the dusty main *allée* leading down to the Musée du Louvre. There's plenty to see and do here, with dozens of statues, ice-cream stands, ponds, and shaded tables where you can stretch out and have a rest. For more information, see "Jardin des Tuileries" on p 90. ⏱ *20 min. Summer daily 7am–9pm; winter daily 7am–8pm. Métro: Tuileries or Concorde.*

**3 ★★★ Musée d'Orsay.** Depending on where you exit the Tuileries, cross the river on the pont de Solterino and turn left, or on the pont Royal and turn right. Walk along the river (enjoying lovely views of the Jardin des Tuileries) until you reach the Gare d'Orsay, the old Beaux Arts train station built for a 1900 exposition and later turned into a museum devoted to works created from 1848 to 1914. It's a must-see for anyone, but fans of Impressionism will be in paradise.

*A fountain in Place de la Concorde.*

## The Musée d'Orsay

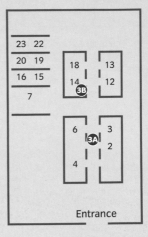

**Top Floor**

**Ground Floor**

Entrance

*Open-air Terrace*

A huge, ornate clock dominates the light-filled central hall. Statues of robust maidens and eager men by Rude, Barye, and Carrier-Belleuse (all 19th-c. sculptors) stand where the train tracks once lay. Those by Carpeaux, including ③A **La Danse** (once controversial for its frolicking nude figures), are extraordinary. Nearby, in ③B **Room 14,** is Manet's striking *Déjeuner sur l'herbe (Picnic on the Grass),* a painting of a graceful nude woman picnicking with fully clothed men that shocked respectable society when it was first exhibited. Upstairs in ③C **Room 32,** Renoir's joyous *Moulin de la Galette* hangs near the jaundiced cafe-goers in Degas's 1876 *Absinthe* (one of his most repro-duced works). Monet fans

should head straight to ③D **Room 39.** Degas's tiny ballerinas twirl for the crowds and their cameras in ③E **Room 31.** Van Gogh's bittersweet *Starry Night* can barely be seen through the crowds of fans in ③F **Room 35.** ⏱ *2–3 hr. Go early in the morning or in the late afternoon to avoid long lines. 1 rue de la Légion d'Honneur, 7th.* ☎ *01-40-49-48-14. www.musee-orsay.fr. Admis-sion 9€. (You can buy tickets in advance from the kiosk on the piazza on the Seine side of the building.) Tues–Wed & Fri–Sat 10am–6pm (from 9am June–Sept); Thurs 10am–9:45pm; Sun 9am–6pm. Métro: Solférino. RER: Musée d'Orsay.*

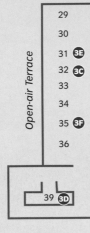

*The clock that graces the museum's central hall.*

*Pont Neuf.*

**4** ★ **Café des Hauteurs.** Take a break over fresh baguette sandwiches and onion soup in the **Musée d'Orsay**'s bustling top-floor cafe. In the summer, eat out on the balcony to take in views of the Seine. Indulge your sweet tooth with a slice of rich chocolate cake. *$*

**5** ★★★ **Ile de la Cité.** When the weather's fine, one of the most Parisian things you can do is stroll along the Seine to the Ile de la Cité. Take a right as you leave the museum. It's about a 15-minute stroll down to this island, home to Notre-Dame Cathedral and the place where Paris was founded. Cross onto the island at the pont Neuf, the oldest bridge in the city (1578), and one of the world's great gathering spots. Jazz musicians, accordion players (unfortunately amplified), and mimes mingle with flirting, giggling Parisian teenagers and tourists capturing the scene on film. On the island, tall, 19th-century buildings keep the narrow streets in perpetual shadow. ⏱ *30 min. Most of the action happens in the early afternoon. You can have it all to yourself first thing in the morning. Free admission. Métro: Pont Neuf.*

**6** ★★ **La Conciergerie.** The towers that soar above the north end of the island near the pont Neuf lead you to the fortress where Marie Antoinette was imprisoned before her execution. Its intimidating look is largely courtesy of an 1850s makeover, but most of the building is much older—one tower dates to the 12th century, another to 1350. Many people were tortured and executed here, and it became a symbol of terror during the French Revolution. You can visit cells in which prisoners were held (including Marie Antoinette's), as well as the towers and former banquet halls. The mood is somber, as if the memory of what took place here has permeated the stones. ⏱ *45 min. 1 quai de l'Horloge, 1st.* ☎ *01-53-40-60-93. www.monum.fr. Admission 6.10€, free for kids under 18. Daily 9:30am–6pm. Métro: Cité.*

**7** ★★★ **Cathédrale de Notre-Dame.** Wind your way to the southern tip of the island to see the familiar silhouette of one of the world's most famous churches. Inevitably, a crowd gathers outside (people dragging wooden crosses, latter-day punks smoking cigarettes, visitors by the hundreds), and this phenomenon—as if the church were a rock star, surrounded by adoring fans—is an attraction in itself.

## Notre-Dame de Paris

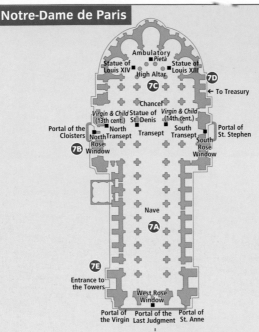

At the far end of the **7A nave** are three elaborately sculpted 13th-century portals: on the left the Portal of the Virgin, in the center the Portal of the Last Judgment, and on the right the Portal of St. Anne. Above them all glow the ruby hues of the West Rose Window, its beauty surpassed only by the **7B North Rose Window.** The colors are especially vivid in the late afternoon. Near the altar is the 14th-century **7C Virgin and Child.** In the **7D treasury,** you'll find a collection of crosses, reliquaries, and ancient gold crowns. To get an up-close look at

the cathedral's famous gargoyles you must climb 67m (223 ft.) up the **7E tower** on old stone staircases—a strenuous workout, but the non-agoraphobic will love the views of the fanciful and detailed hobgoblins, devils, and birds of prey. ⏱ *2 hr. 6 place du parvis Notre-Dame, 4th.* ☎ *01-42-34-56-10. www. paris.org/monuments/ ndame. Admission free to cathedral, 6.10€ to tower, 3€ to treasury. Cathedral: daily 8am–6:45pm. Tower & crypt: Apr–Sept daily 9:30am–6pm; Oct–Mar daily 10am–5:15pm. Treasury: Mon–Sat 9:30am–6pm, Sun 2–6pm. Métro: Cité.*

One of Notre-Dame's many gargoyles.

*Floating along the Seine on a* bateau mouche.

**8** ★ **Le Flore en l'Isle.** Escape the crowds by crossing pont St-Louis, behind Notre-Dame, to tiny Ile St-Louis. Several cafes near the bridge have excellent views of the cathedral's famous flying buttresses. Le Flore is one of the best cafes on the island for ice cream and sorbet. *42 quai d'Orleans, 4th.* ☎ *01-43-29-88-27.* $

**9** ★★ **Relaxing in St-Germain.** Retrace your steps back across the Ile de la Cité and continue to the Left Bank. Turn left on rue de la Cité and cross the bridge into the bustle of St-Germain-des-Prés. This area was the incubator for artistic creativity in the 1920s, for Nazi resistance in the 1940s, and for student revolution in the 1960s. These days, you can get a great cup of coffee, drop a wad of money on high-fashion clothes, or spend a night on the town. The best way to experience the neighborhood is to wander along glittering, tree-lined boulevard St-Germain, soaking up the atmosphere and stopping at shops and bars that spark your fancy. My favorite cafes include the stylish **Café de Flore,** 172 bd. St-Germain (☎ 01-45-48-55-26), a favorite of the philosopher Jean-Paul Sartre; and the more touristy **Les Deux Magots,** 6 place St-Germain-des-Prés

*Café de Flore, in St-Germain.*

(☎ 01-45-48-55-26), a regular haunt of both Sartre and Hemingway. At either spot you can linger over a café au lait (5€), or enjoy a complete meal (16€–28€).

**10** ★★ **Riding a *Bateau Mouche.*** If you have any energy left after dinner, walk down to the riverside at the pont Neuf and catch one of Bateaux Vedettes' long, low boats known as *bateaux mouches.* By night, the boats glow with lights as they navigate the river, offering magical views of Paris. ⏲ *1 hr. Square du Vert Galant, 4th.* ☎ *01-46-33-98-38. www.pontneuf.net. Tickets 9€. Mar–Oct about every 30 min. daily 10:30am–10:30pm. Nov–Feb about every 45 min. daily 10:30am–10pm.*

# The Best **in Two Days**

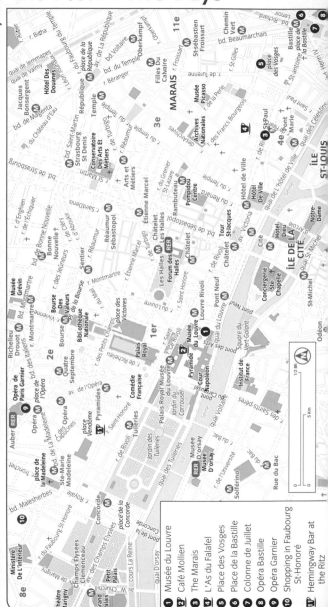

1 Musée du Louvre
2 Café Mollien
3 The Marais
4 L'As du Falafel
5 Place des Vosges
6 Place de la Bastille
7 Colonne de Juillet
8 Opéra Bastille
9 Opéra Garnier
10 Shopping in Faubourg St-Honoré
TP Hemingway Bar at the Ritz

If you followed the 1-day tour of Paris you've already had a good introduction to the city, but there's obviously lots more to see. You may want to start your day early with a coffee and a fresh croissant from a *boulangerie*—I love Poilâne, 8 rue du Cherche-Miki (☎ 01-45-48-42-59), in the Latin Quarter, not far from the Louvre.
**START: Métro to the Louvre**

**①** ★★★ **Musée du Louvre.** You have to arrive early to catch the best views and the shortest lines at this, arguably the world's greatest, art museum. The lines here rival those at Disneyland, but it's worth it—you've never seen a museum like this one, in terms of the sheer depth of its collection. With your ticket in hand, you must decide whether to brave the crowds in front of the *Mona Lisa* or to seek out less famous works in hopes of a little peace. For help navigating the museum, see the **Louvre tour** on p 26. ⏱ *3 hr. Arrive shortly after opening; avoid weekends & holidays. 34–36 quai du Louvre, 1st; entrance in the glass pyramid in the main courtyard.* ☎ *01-40-20-53-17. www.louvre.fr. Admission 8.50€ (free for children under 18, free for everyone 1st Sun of each month). Tues–Sun 9am–6pm. Métro: Palais Royal–Musée du Louvre.*

**②** ★★ **Café Mollien.** The Louvre is so big that I barely make it from the Métro to the ticket office without needing a rest, and I always need a coffee or lunch break at some point. I prefer Café Mollien to other Louvre cafes because of its terrace and fresh sandwiches. *$*

**③** ★★ **The Marais.** After the Louvre, my brain is always on culture overload, and I'm ready for something a little different. If you take the Métro from Louvre Rivoli to St Paul, you'll find exactly that. The winding medieval streets of the Marais—traditionally the city's old Jewish quarter—curl past magnificent mansions (called *hôtels*), charming boutiques, tiny Jewish bakeries, and personable ethnic restaurants. You can spend hours perusing its little shops and small, absorbing museums if you take the **Marais tour** (p 64). ⏱ *2 hr. Early weekday afternoons are best. Everything is closed on Sat, the Jewish Sabbath. Métro: St-Paul.*

**④** ★ **L'As du Falafel.** This is one of my favorite lunch places in Paris. This tiny cafe, with a window for takeout orders, makes the best falafel sandwiches (4€) in the city. Unless it's raining I get mine to go, and eat them on a bench in nearby place des Vosges. (See next stop.) *34 rue des Rosiers, 4th.* ☎ *01-48-87-63-60. $*

*An artist finds inspiration at the Louvre.*

*Place des Vosges.*

circle with a column at the center. But I think it's worth a stop to see the place where the ideals of democracy found symbolic expression. 🕐 *15 min. Métro: Bastille.*

**7** ★ **Colonne de Juillet.** It was probably easier to storm the Bastille than it is to cross the traffic to the center of place de la Bastille for a close-up view of this lovely memorial. A bit ironically, given its location, this column honors the victims of the 1830 revolution, which put Louis-Philippe on the throne after the upheaval of the Napoleonic wars. The glittering statue on top of the tall pedestal is Liberty giving away a crown. 🕐 *A few min. Place de la Bastille, 4th. Métro: Bastille.*

**8** ★ **Opéra Bastille.** This impossible-to-miss behemoth (it has been compared to a beached whale), which opened in 1989, is the home of the Opéra National de Paris. It's clear that the designer of the building, Carlos Ott, paid a lot of attention to its appearance, but music lovers say it would have been nice if acoustics had been taken into consideration, too. If you take in a show, you'll get to see designer Issey Miyake's stage curtain, although it's not much to write home about, to be honest. 🕐 *15 min. 2 place de la Bastille, 4th.* ☎ *01-40-01-17-89. Tickets 20€–114€. Métro: Bastille.*

**9** ★★ **Opéra Garnier.** Now go see what opera used to look like in Paris. You can either hop back on the Métro and take it to Opéra, or take a taxi to this architectural explosion, which goes beyond baroque and well into rococo. This was the city's main opera house until Opéra Bastille came along, but now it also hosts dance performances beneath an elaborate false ceiling painted by Chagall in 1964. The facade is all marble and flowing sculpture, with gilded busts,

**5** ★ **Place des Vosges.** I am in love with this place. This is Paris's oldest square, and its most unusual—it is perfectly symmetrical, formed by 36 red-brick-and-stone arcades with sharply pitched roofs. It's surrounded by shops, and the atmosphere is fabulously Paris. If you're looking for art to take home, check out **Deborah Chock** at 20 place des Vosges, which sells the unique contemporary paintings of its namesake artist. Most are oil on canvas with a very modern emphasis. 🕐 *30 min. Métro: Bastille.*

**6** ★ **Place de la Bastille.** It's a very short walk to rue St Antoine, which leads you to the site of one of the most famous moments in French revolutionary history. Here stood the Bastille prison, a massive building that loomed ominously over the city. On July 14, 1789, a mob attacked it, freeing all of France from the tyranny of its presence. Today, the site is not so impressive—it's a busy traffic

*Opéra Garnier.*

multihued pillars, and vivid mosaics. This is where the Phantom did his haunting, and for the price of a ticket you can wander its halls too.
🕐 *20 min. Place de l'Opera, 9th.*
☎ *01-40-01-17-89. Tickets 23€–114€. Métro: Opéra.*

**⑩ ★★ Shopping in Faubourg St-Honoré.** Well, since you're here . . . Opéra Garnier is smack-dab in the middle of France's most exclusive shopping area, simply called "the Faubourg" by those in the know. Start anywhere, and you're sure to find something you love. Try **Alain Figaret** (21 rue de la Paix) for men's shirts and women's blouses; **Charvet** (28 place Vendôme) for custom-made clothes; or **Cherry Chau** (87 passage de Choiseul) for affordable handmade jewelry. About a 15-minute walk away is the **Annexe des Créateurs** (19 rue Godot de Mauroy)—a fabulous discount shop for designer fashions (Versace, Moschino, Gaultier . . . ). Another 15-minute walk takes you to the

oh-so-French makeup and perfume at **Guerlain** (68 av. des Champs-Elysées) and **Sephora** (70 av. des Champs-Elysées). 🕐 *2 hr. Métro: Opéra.*

**⑪ ★★★ Hemingway Bar at the Ritz.** After a long day traversing the city, a drink might be in order. The dark wood, leather chairs, photos of Papa everywhere, and charm of the bar staff make this one of the best bars in Paris—this is what expat living is all about. Drinks, though, are outrageously expensive (23€ for a raspberry martini). *Hotel Ritz, 15 place Vendôme, 1st.* ☎ *01-43-16-30-31. www.ritzparis. com. Open Tues–Sat 6:30pm–2am. Closed July 25–Aug 25. Métro: Madeleine or Concorde.*

*A raspberry martini from the Hemingway Bar.*

# The Best **in Three Days**

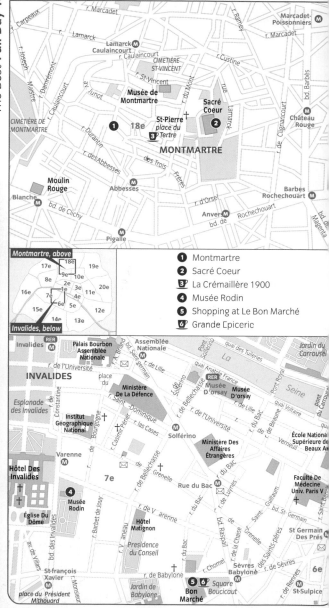

**Montmartre, above**

17e 18e
16e 8e 9e 10e 19e
2e 3e
1e 4e 11e 20e
7e 6e 5e
15e 12e
14e 13e

**Invalides, below**

❶ Montmartre
❷ Sacré Coeur
**3'** La Crémaillère 1900
❹ Musée Rodin
❺ Shopping at Le Bon Marché
**6'** Grande Epiceric

**Y**ou've been running around like a crazy person for 2 days, so today you may want to slow down a bit. Stop and smell the roses. Get a new perspective—from the top of a hill, say. A very steep hill. Take the time to tilt at a few windmills. And, frankly, some of you really haven't done enough shopping yet. START: **Métro to Abesses or place Blanche**

**❶ ★★★ Montmartre.** With its steep hills, staircase streets, quaint windmills, and sweeping views, this is the most romantic neighborhood in Paris, and many would say the most beautiful. Unfortunately, it's not exactly a secret—prepare yourself for some tacky souvenir shops and the ever-present tourist onslaught around the Sacré Coeur. Still, spending a morning wandering around the streets of Montmartre is enough to make the heart flutter (and not just from the exertion of climbing all those stairs). Take the Métro to Abesses or place Blanche, and head upward. Fall in love with streets like rue des Abesses, rue des Trois Frères, or rue des Martyres. Find the windmills on rue LePic, or the racier one atop the still-titillating Moulin Rouge. For more guidance, try the Montmartre walking tour on p 68. ⏱ *2 hr. Métro: Abesses or Place Blanche*.

**❷ ★★★ Sacré Coeur.** You can either take a funicular up from the end of rue Berthe or, better still, wander up via hustling place du Tertre; however you get here, this white, wedding-cake cathedral will draw a gasp from you when it first hovers into view. Construction began in 1876, and didn't end until 1919—the whole thing was paid for by donations from the faithful. The mosaics inside—on the ceiling, the walls, and the floors—are almost dizzying, and the panoramic view from the steps out front is almost as splendid as the one from its dome. ⏱ *1 hr. Place St-Pierre, 18th.* ☎ *01-53-41-89-00. www.paris.org/ Monuments/Sacre-Coeur. Admission free to basilica; dome & crypt 5€. Daily 6am–11pm. Métro: Abesses.*

**❸ ★★ La Crémaillère 1900.** Most of the restaurants around the place du Tertre near the Sacré Coeur are tourist traps, but this is an exception. Its Belle Epoque dining room is filled with art, and you can enjoy classical French cuisine while sitting on a terrace that opens onto the square. *15 place du Tertre, 18th.* ☎ *01-46-06-58-59. $$*

*Sacré Coeur.*

The Thinker, *in the courtyard of the Musée Rodin.*

**4** ★★ **Musée Rodin.** A short Métro ride will bring you to this peaceful museum, where the sculptor Auguste Rodin once had his studio. Today his works are scattered inside and outside a somber 18th-century mansion of gray stone. *The Thinker* perches pensively in the courtyard, while the lovers in *Le Baiser* kiss in perpetuity inside. There's also a room devoted to the oft-overlooked works of Rodin's talented mistress, Camille Claudel. ⏱ *1 hr.; it's rarely crowded, so it's a good option when things are busy at the Louvre. Hôtel Biron, 77 rue de Varenne, 7th.* ☎ *01-44-18-61-10. www.musee-rodin.fr. Admission 5€, free for kids under 18. Apr–Sept Tues–Sun 9:30am–5:45pm; Oct–Mar Tues–Sun 9:30am-4:45pm. Métro: Varenne.*

**5** ★ **Shopping at Le Bon Marché.** If you haven't found everything you hoped to yet, and you're tired of walking from boutique to boutique, do what the locals do and come to this swank department store. The "Balthazar" section is a clutch of designer boutiques for men, and the "Theater of Beauty" is one for the ladies. It's all very Chanel, which may put some strains on the holiday budget. But it's Paris's oldest department store, and even the elevator is designer, so you should at least have a look. ⏱ *2 hr. 24 rue de Sèvres, 7th.* ☎ *01-44-39-80-00. www.bonmarche.fr. Mon–Sat 9:30am–7pm. Métro: Sèvres-Babylone.*

**6** ★ **Grande Epicerie.** In a building connected to the Bon Marché, this grand food hall contains all the pâtés and cheeses your heart could desire. You can build yourself a gorgeous picnic, or take a seat in the excellent bar and restaurant and let someone else do all the work. ☎ *01-44-39-81-00. www.lagrande epicerie.fr. $$* ●

*Emile Zola's novel* The Ladies' Paradise *is based on Le Bon Marché and its founders, the Boucicauts.*

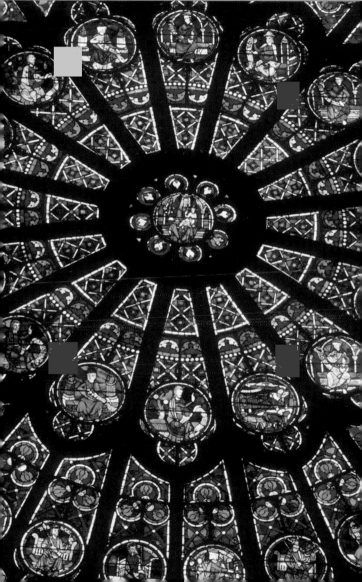

# Monumental Paris

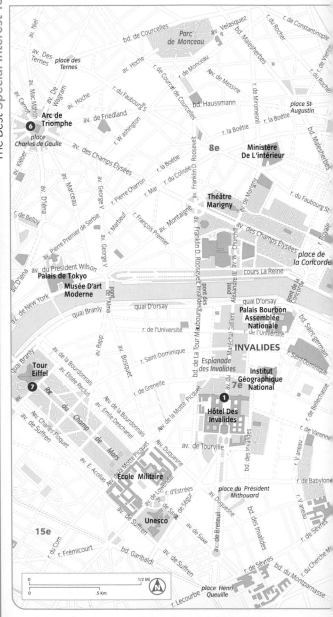

r. Niel
bd. de Courcelles
Parc de Monceau
av. Velasquez
bd. Malesherbes
r. du Rocher
r. de Constantinople
r. de Vienne
r. du Rocher

av. Des Ternes
place des Ternes
av. Hoche
r. de Courcel
de Courcelles
r. de Monceau
av. de Messine
r. de Miromesnil
bd. Haussmann
place St-Augustin

av. Mac Mahon
av. De Wagram
av. Hoche
r. du Faubourg St
r. la Boétie
r. la Boétie
bd. Malesherbes

av. Carnot
**6** **Arc de Triomphe**
place Charles de Gaulle
av. de Friedland
av. W. Washington
**8e**
**Ministère De L'intérieur**

av. Kléber
av. des Champs Élysées
r. la Boétie
r. du Colisée
av. Franklin D. Roosevelt

av. Marceau
av. George V
r. Pierre Charron
r. Mar
**Théâtre Marigny**
r. de Marigny
r. du Faubourg St-

r. d'Iéna
av. Pierre Premier de Serbie
r. Marbeuf
av. Montaigne
av. des Champs Élysées
av. W. Churchill
Royale

r. de Belloy
av. George V
r. François Premier
**place de la Concorde**

av. du President Wilson
cours La Reine
av. d'Iéna
**Palais de Tokyo**
**Musée D'art Moderne**
pont de l'Alma
quai D'orsay
pont Alexandre III
pont de la Concorde

av. de New York
quai Branly
quai D'orsay
**Palais Bourbon**
bd. Saint-germain

quai Branly
av. de la Bourdonnais
av. de Suffren
r. de l'Université
**Assemblée Nationale**
r. de l'Université
r. Saint-germain

av. Rapp
av. Bosquet
r. Saint-Dominique
bd. De La Tour Maubourg
**INVALIDES**
r. Saint-Dominique

quai Branly
**7** **Tour Eiffel**
Parc
av. de la Bourdonnais
av. Elisée Reclus
**Esplanade des Invalides**
av. du
**Institut Géographique National**
r. de Bellechasse

av. Charles Floquet
av. de Suffren
du
Champ
av. Emile Deschanel
**1**
**7e**
r. de Varenne

av. E. Acollas
de Mors
av. de la Motte Picquet
**Hôtel Des Invalides**

av. de Suffren
r. de Grenelle
**École Militaire**
av. de Lowendal
av. de Ségur
av. d'Estrées
av. de Tourville
bd. des Invalides
V. aneau

**15e**
av. de Suffren
r. d'Estrées
**place du Président Mithouard**
av. Duquesne
r. de Babylone

**Unesco**
av. de Saxe
av. de Breteuil
bd. des Invalides
r. de Sèvres

r. du Com.
r. Frémicourt
bd. Garibaldi
av. de Suffren
av. de Saxe
r. de Sèvres
bd. du Montparnasse
r. du Cherche Mi

0 ——— 1/2 Mi
0 ——— .5 Km
**place Henri Queuille**
r. Lecourbe

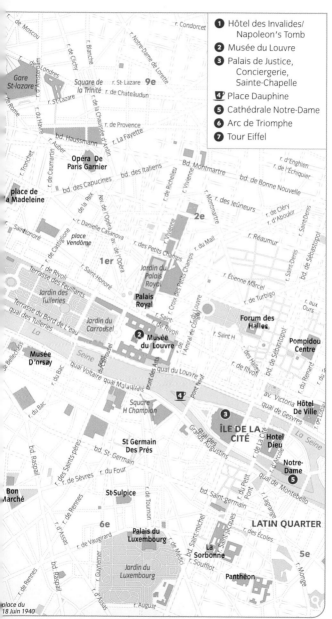

1. Hôtel des Invalides/ Napoleon's Tomb
2. Musée du Louvre
3. Palais de Justice, Conciergerie, Sainte-Chapelle
4. Place Dauphine
5. Cathédrale Notre-Dame
6. Arc de Triomphe
7. Tour Eiffel

**T**his tour covers a lot of ground, so prepare for a busy day. For your efforts, you'll see the city's most glorious edifices all at one go. If you get an early start and keep moving, you should be able to make it to the Eiffel Tower (the last stop) by sunset. START: **Métro to Invalides**

**1** ★★★ **Hôtel des Invalides/ Napoleon's Tomb.** As tombs go, this one is pretty impressive—trust Napoleon to have only the best. It was built in 1670 as a home for injured or disabled soldiers, thus its size. Its beauty—with a gilded dome and symmetrical corridors—well, that's just the French for you. Approach it from the Invalides Métro station to see it as intended, from the end of its perfectly balanced gardens. Inside, along with accouterments of Napoleon's life and death, is the Musée de l'Armée, with enough historic weaponry (vicious battle axes, clumsy blunderbusses) to mount a low-tech revolution. Among the collection's gems are suits of armor worn by the kings and dignitaries of France, including one worn by Louis XIV and François I's "armor suit of the lion." Henri II ordered his suit engraved with the monograms of both his mistress, Diane de Poitiers, and his wife, Catherine de Médicis. The museum also contains World War I mementos like the Armistice Bugle, which sounded the cease-fire. Napoleon's

*Hôtel des Invalides, which houses Napoleon's tomb and an armory museum.*

over-the-top tomb features giant statues that represent his victories surrounding his famously tiny body. You can also see his death mask and an oil by Delaroche, painted at the time of Napoleon's first banishment in 1814. 🕐 *1 hr. Place des Invalides,*

*Napoleon's tomb.*

*7th.* ☎ *01-44-42-37-72. Admission 7€, free for kids under 18. Oct–Mar daily 10am–5pm; Apr–May, Sept daily 10am–6pm; June–Aug daily 10am–7pm. Métro: Invalides.*

### ❷ ★★★ Musée du Louvre.

This was once the world's largest royal palace. In 1527, François I demolished most of the old castle to build a new one, which makes up part of the building you see today—what remains of François's palace is called the Vieux Louvre, or "Old Louvre." (François also founded the museum's collection—the *Mona Lisa* and *Virgin of the Rocks* once hung in his bathroom.) The rest of the building was completed over centuries, and the monograms of Henri II, his wife Catherine de Médici, and his mistress Diane du Poitiers are hidden in the elaborate carvings along the front of the facade. The long gallery (where the *Mona Lisa* is now) was first used as a museum in 1793, and the glass pyramids designed by I. M. Pei arrived with a great flurry of architectural unrest in 1989. In order to complete the rest of this tour, save your visit of the art collection for another day. (See p 26 for the **Louvre tour**.) ⏱ *45 min. 34–36 quai du Louvre, 1st.* ☎ *01-40-20-53-17. www.louvre.fr. Access to the museum grounds is free. Métro: Palais Royal–Musée du Louvre.*

### ❸ ★★★ Palais de Justice, Conciergerie & Sainte-Chapelle.

Walk east along the river to pont Neuf—the bridge to Ile de la Cité. Turn left after you cross the bridge and you'll see the complex made up of the Palais de Justice (law courts), the Conciergerie (formerly a prison, now a museum), and the exquisite Sainte-Chapelle. The Palais is still the center of the French judicial system, and it's worth a peek inside at its grand lobby. Once a palace, the Conciergerie was converted to a prison during the Revolution and became a symbol of terror—Paris's answer to the Tower of London. Carts once frequently pulled up to the Conciergerie to haul off fresh victims for the guillotine. Among the few imprisoned here who lived to tell the tale was American political theorist and writer Thomas Paine. Inside, you can learn about the bloody history of the Conciergerie and visit some of the old prison cells, including Marie Antoinette's. The Sainte-Chapelle—stunning in afternoon light—was built in the 13th century to hold a crown of thorns that King Louis IX believed Christ wore during his crucifixion. The chapel's 15 stained-glass windows comprise over 1,000 scenes depicting the Christian story from the Garden of Eden through the Apocalypse, depicted on the great Rose Window. (Read them from bottom to top and from left to right.) The stained glass of Sainte-Chapelle is magnificent in daylight, glowing with reds that have inspired the saying "wine the color of Sainte-Chapelle's windows." ⏱ *1 hr. 1 quai de l'Horloge, 1st.* ☎ *01-53-40-60-93. www.monum.fr. Free admission to the grounds & Palais de Justice; Conciergerie 6.10€; Sainte-Chapelle 6.10€. Free for kids under 18 for both. Daily 9:30am–6pm. Métro: Cité.*

*Sainte-Chapelle's stained-glass windows.*

*The Arc de Triomphe stands about 49m (161 ft.) high and 44m (144 ft.) wide.*

**4** ★ **Place Dauphine.** This tiny square sits where the pont Neuf reaches the island. It's filled with restaurants and cafes, any of which makes a good stop for lunch. If you've brought a picnic lunch and the day is sunny, you can spread it in the grass and eat here, with a view of the water, and the towers of the Conciergerie overhead. $–$$

**5** ★★★ **Cathédrale Notre-Dame.** For a good view of the buttresses, take the short bridge just behind the cathedral to Ile St-Louis. ⏱ *1 hr. See p 9, bullet* **7**.

*Formidable Notre-Dame, where Napoleon crowned himself emperor.*

**6** ★★★ **Arc de Triomphe.** The world's largest triumphal arch was commissioned by Napoleon in 1806 to commemorate the victories of his Grand Armée. The monument is engraved with the names of hundreds of generals (those underlined died in battle) who commanded French troops in Napoleonic victories. The arch was finished in 1836, after Napoleon's death. His remains, brought from St. Helena in 1840, passed under it on their journey to his final resting place at the Hôtel des Invalides. These days the arch is the focal point of state funerals, and the site of the tomb of the Unknown Soldier, in whose honor an eternal flame burns. It's also a huge traffic circle, representing certain death to pedestrians, so you reach the arch via an underground passage (well signposted). The constant roar of traffic can ruin the mood, but the view from the top (accessible via elevator or stairs) makes enduring the din worthwhile. If you can, flag down a taxi on the Champs Elysées for the last leg of your tour. (If not, hop back on the Métro to Trocadéro.) ⏱ *45 min. The Arc de Triomphe is open late at night, so if you prefer a nighttime view, you can put this off*

*until after dinner. Place Charles de Gaulle–Etoile, 8th.* ☎ *01-55-37-73-77. www.monum.fr. Admission 7€; 4.50€ for those 18–25; free for kids under 18. Apr–Sept daily 10am–11pm; Oct–Mar daily 10am–10:30pm. Métro: Charles de Gaulle–Etoile.*

**7** ★★★ **Tour Eiffel.** At last. It's the Eiffel Tower to us and the *Tour Eiffel* to the rest of the world, but whatever you call it, it is synonymous with Paris. The tower was meant to be temporary, built by Gustave-Alexandre Eiffel (who also created the framework for the Statue of Liberty) in 1889 for the Universal Exhibition. It weighs 7,000 tons but exerts about the same pressure on the ground as an average-size person sitting in a chair. Praised by some and denounced by others, the tower created as much controversy in the 1880s as I. M. Pei's glass pyramid at the Louvre did in the 1980s. The tower, including

A table at Le Jules Verne, in the Eiffel Tower.

*The Eiffel Tower was once denounced as the "world's greatest lamppost."*

its TV antenna, is 317m (1,040 ft.) high, and from the top you can see for 65km (40 miles). But the view *of* the tower is just as important as the view *from* it. If you go to Trocadéro on the Métro, then walk from the Palais de Chaillot gardens across the Seine, you'll get the best view (not to mention photo opportunities). I always come right at sunset or just after dark, to see Paris sparkling below me. Inside the tower's lacy ironwork are restaurants, bars, and historic memorabilia. Take your time, have a drink, or even book a table at pricey restaurant Le Jules Verne (☎ 01-45-55-61-44), and enjoy sweeping views from the second level as you dine. ⏱ *2 hr. Champ de Mars, 7th.* ☎ *01-44-11-23-23. www.tour-eiffel.fr. Admission: 1st landing 3.70€; 2nd landing 7€; 3rd landing 10€. Sept–May daily 9:30am–11pm; June–Aug daily 9am–midnight. Métro: Trocadéro, Ecole Militaire, or Bir-Hakeim.*

# Exploring the Louvre

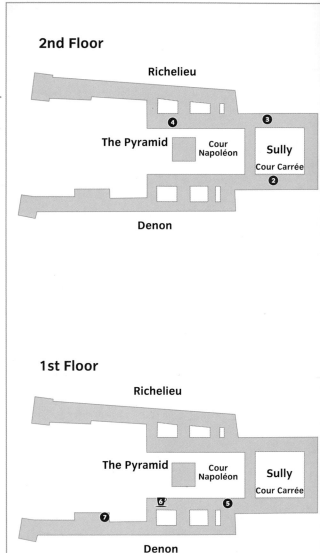

**2nd Floor**

Richelieu

The Pyramid

Cour Napoléon

Sully

Cour Carrée

Denon

**1st Floor**

Richelieu

The Pyramid

Cour Napoléon

Sully

Cour Carrée

Denon

1. *Venus de Milo*
2. The *Turkish Bath*
3. *The Cheat with the Ace of Diamonds*
4. *The Lacemaker*
5. *Winged Victory of Samothrace*
6. Café Mollien
7. *Mona Lisa*
8. Italian Sculpture

## Ground Floor

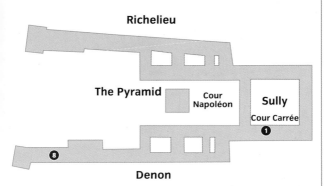

**Richelieu**

**The Pyramid**  Cour Napoléon  **Sully**

Cour Carrée

**1**

**8**

**Denon**

## The Pyramid

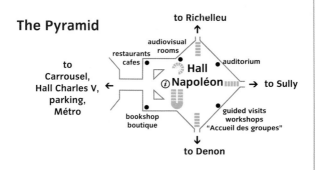

to Richelieu

audiovisual rooms

restaurants cafes

to Carrousel, Hall Charles V, parking, Métro

**Hall Napoléon**

*i*

auditorium

→ to Sully

bookshop boutique

guided visits workshops "Accueil des groupes"

to Denon

This tour is designed to help you dip your toe into the Louvre's sea of art. It's impossible to see everything in a day, so I've chosen some of my favorites, some crowd pleasers, and a few hidden gems. To see the rest, you'll just have to come back again and again. Allow 3 to 4 hours to see everything on this tour and to do a little browsing between stops. **START: Métro to Palais Royal–Musée du Louvre**

❶ ★★★ *Venus de Milo.* Begin your tour in Greek Antiquities, where Venus stands alluringly, her drapery about to fall to the floor. The statue dates to 100 B.C. Myths about her abound—one story maintains that her arms were knocked off when she was hustled onto a French ship. Another claims she was rescued from a pottery kiln. Both are untrue—she was found buried as you see her now, along with part of an arm, a hand holding an apple, and a pair of small columns, one of which fit neatly into her base and bore the inscription ALEXANDROS, SON OF MENIDES, CITIZEN OF ANTIOCH, MADE THIS STATUE. Sadly, those parts were all lost over time. *Room 12.*

❷ ★ The *Turkish Bath.* Take the stairs to the third floor (which, confusingly, the French would call the second floor) to see the titillating lush nudity of A. D. Ingres's *Turkish Bath.* Ingres was a popular French

*Venus de Milo, one of the Louvre's most popular works of art.*

*Vermeer's* The Lacemaker.

painter in the early 19th century, and this erotic idealized painting of overly friendly women lounging in a (very crowded) bath was the masterwork of his final years. *Room 60.*

❸ ★★ *The Cheat with the Ace of Diamonds.* Retrace your steps back to the staircase and then past it, turn right at the corner, and go to Room 30. In this gorgeous work (1630) by Georges de la Tour, complex relationships play out in shimmering colors. In the center, a courtesan holds her hand out for a glass of wine poured by a servant. Her cheating friend holds cards behind his back as she casts a colluding glance at him. The chubby-cheeked youth in the embroidered shirt is the victim of a plot. A cruel tale, playfully told. *Room 30.*

**❹ ★★★ The Lacemaker.** As you follow the hallway to the Richelieu Wing and straight on through the 14th-century French paintings, pause for a glance at the extraordinary portrait of John II in Room 1 on your way to *The Lacemaker,* one of my favorites. This delightful little painting (1664) by Johannes Vermeer shows a young woman bent over her work, her shape forming a subtle pyramid, and her face, hair, and rich yellow blouse aglow. Vermeer's unique use of color and light are exemplified in this work, which is usually surrounded by a crowd of admirers. *Room 38.*

**❺ ★ Winged Victory of Samothrace.** Take the escalator down to the second floor and head back toward the Sully Wing, stopping first in Room 25 to take in the strange little statue of the gnome riding a snail. Turn right at Room 34 and dash past the stairs through the bronzes, turning right into the Denon Wing. At the top of the Daru stairs stands Nike, the goddess of

Winged Victory of Samothrace *(sometimes called* Nike of Samothrace*)*.

victory, her wings flung back in takeoff, and the fabric of her skirts swirling around her, as fine as silk. The statue's origins are uncertain. Most scholars date it to somewhere between 220 and 190 B.C. The statue was discovered on the Greek

## Louvre Survival Tips

This is one of the world's biggest museums, but there's no way words on a page can convey its size. Stretched out end to end, it would be the size of several football fields. With stairs. I always tackle it by choosing a few works I really want to see, and then aiming in their general direction. This helps me maintain my focus. Otherwise I could end up like one of those people staggering randomly through the Medieval France section muttering, "But it's all so beautiful . . ." and never find the Vermeer I hoped to see. You can avoid this fate by getting a museum map in the ticket hall and keeping it handy. All the rooms are numbered, so when you get lost (not, you'll notice, *if*), you can find your way back. At the same time, don't get too carried away with the whole focus thing. Take some time to look for new favorites along the way. And if you do end up wandering amid French medieval paintings (Richelieu Wing, third floor), well, things could be worse.

island of Samothrace in 1863, and its base was discovered in 1879. In 1950, one of the statue's hands was found; it's on display in a glass case near the statue. An inscription on the statue's base includes the word RHODHIOS (Rhodes) and this, along with the fact that the statue stands on the prow of a ship, has led some scholars to theorize that the statue was commissioned in celebration of a naval victory by Rhodes. Others believe the statue was an offering made by a Macedonian general after a victory in Cyprus. Regardless of its origins, this glorious work is considered one of the best surviving Greek sculptures from that period. *Top of the Daru staircase.*

*The* Mona Lisa *once hung over François I's bathtub.*

6 ★ **Café Mollien.** Ready for a break? Café Mollien is particularly enjoyable in the summertime when the outdoor terrace is open. The café au lait is good here, as is the fresh smoked-salmon sandwich. *Off Rooms 75 & 77.*

7 ★★★ **Mona Lisa.** It's a long way to the end of the Denon Wing and the hiding place of one of the world's most famous paintings, but everybody makes the trip. The enigmatic smile, the challenging eyes, the endless debates (Was she the wife of an Italian city official? Is she meant to be in mourning? Is "she" a man—perhaps even a self-portrait of da Vinci himself?) continue now as ever. The painting has been through a lot over the years. It was stolen in 1911 (by a Louvre employee who simply

*The Louvre stretches for almost a kilometer (⅗ mile).*

# The Louvre: Practical Matters

The Musée du Louvre (☎ 01-40-20-53-17; www.louvre.fr) is located at 34–36 quai du Louvre, 1st; enter through the glass pyramid in the main courtyard if you need to buy a ticket (and expect a long line). If you have your tickets already (you can buy them in advance online at www.ticketweb.com if you're from the United States or Canada; from http://louvre.francebillet.com or www.ticketnet.fr from other countries), go to the Passage Richelieu entrance, 93 rue de Rivoli.

Admission is 8.50€; it's free for children under 18, and free for everyone the first Sunday of each month. The museum is open Tues, Thurs, Sat, and Sun from 9am to 6pm; and Wed, Fri, 9am to 9:45pm. Arrive early for the best viewing.

put the painting under his coat and walked out with it) and wasn't recovered until 1913. During World War II it was housed in various parts of France for safekeeping. In 1956 the painting was severely damaged after someone threw acid on it. In 1962 and 1963 it toured the United States, and was shown in New York City and Washington, D.C. In 1974 it was shown in Tokyo and Moscow. All the hype and history aside, some find actually seeing Leonardo da Vinci's *Mona Lisa* (painted between 1503 and 1507) a disappointment. It's a very small painting to have caused such a fuss, and has been kept behind glass since it was slashed by a vandal in the 1990s. That, along with the crowds surrounding it, make it difficult to connect with. Despite these shortcomings, few come to the Louvre without stopping by at least once. (In 2006 the painting will move to its own room in the nearby Salle des Etats.) *Room 13.*

**⑧ ★★★ Italian Sculpture.** Make your way down to the ground floor of the Denon Wing and head to Room 4, which is filled with exquisite Italian sculptures. Michelangelo's two statues are among the most dramatic in the room—the muscular arms of his *Rebellious Slave* are tensed furiously against his bindings, while the *Dying Slave* seems resigned to his fate. Both were commissioned in 1505 by Pope Julius as funerary art. Look across the room for the delicate wings of Cupid, who clutches the breast of Psyche in a *pas de deux* in pure white marble in Antonio Canova's *Cupid Awakening Psyche* (1793). It is love carved in stone. *Room 4.*

*According to myth, Cupid awakens Psyche from eternal slumber with a kiss.*

# Gourmet Paris

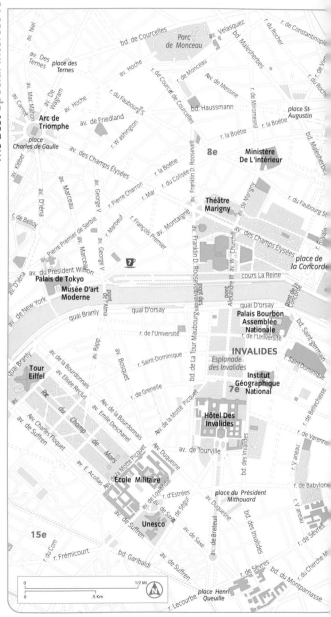

av. Niel
bd. de Courcelles
Parc de Monceau
av. Velasquez
bd. Malesherbes
r. du Rocher
r. de Constantinople
av. Des Ternes
place des Ternes
av. Hoche
r. de Courcelles
r. de Monceau
av. de Messine
r. de Miromesnil
r. de Vienne
r. du Roche
av. De Wagram
av. Hoche
r. du Faubourg S
bd. Haussmann
place St-Augustin
av. Mac Mahon
av. Carnot
Arc de Triomphe
place Charles de Gaulle
av. de Friedland
av. W ashington
r. la Boétie
r. la Boétie
bd. Malesherbe
av. Kléber
av. des Champs Élysées
r. la Boétie
Franklin D. Roosevelt
8e
Ministère De L'intérieur
av. D'Iéna
av. Marceau
av. George V
r. Pierre Charron
r. Mar
r. du Colisée
av. de Marigny
r. du Faubourg St
r. de Belloy
av. Pierre Premier de Serbie
av. Marceau
r. Marbeuf
r. François av. Montaigne
Théâtre Marigny
av. des Champs Élysées
place de la Concorde
av. George V
r. François Premier
av. W. Churchill
pont Alexandre III
pont de la Concorde
av. D'Iéna
av. du President Wilson
Palais de Tokyo
Musée D'art Moderne
pont de l'Alma
cours La Reine
av. de New York
quai Branly
quai D'orsay
quai D'orsay
Palais Bourbon Assemblée Nationale
r. de l'Université
bd. Saint-germain
quai Branly
av. de la Bourdonnais
av. Rapp
av. Bosquet
r. Saint-Dominique
r. de l'Université
r. Saint-Dominique
Tour Eiffel
av. Élisée Reclus
r. de Grenelle
INVALIDES
Esplanade des Invalides
Institut Géographique National
r. de Bellechasse
Parc du Champ de Mars
av. de la Bourdonnais
av. Émile Deschanel
bd. de La Tour Maubourg
7e
av. Charles Floquet
av. de Suffren
av. E. Acollas
av. de la Motte Picquet
Hôtel Des Invalides
av. de Varenne
av. Duquesne
av. de Tourville
bd. des Invalides
Ecole Militaire
av. de Lowendal
r. d'Estrées
av. de Ségur
av. de Saxe
place du Président Mithouard
av. Duquesne
bd. des Invalides
r. de Babylone
av. V aneau
15e
Unesco
av. de Suffren
av. de Breteuil
bd. des Sèvres
r. de Babylone
r. du Com
r. Frémicourt
bd. Garibaldi
av. de Saxe
av. de Suffren
bd. des Sèvres
bd. du Montparnasse
r. de Sèvres
r. du Cherche M
r. Lecourbe
place Henri Queuille
0    1/2 Mi
0    .5 Km

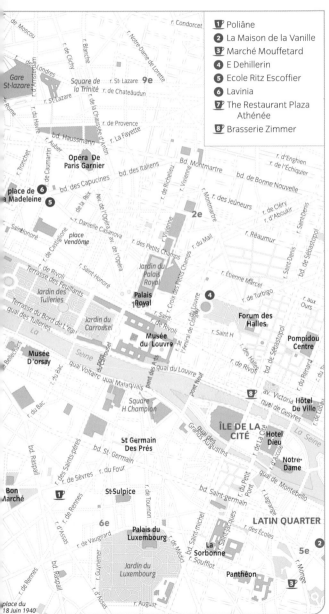

1 Poliâne
2 La Maison de la Vanille
3 Marché Mouffetard
4 E Dehillerin
5 Ecole Ritz Escoffier
6 Lavinia
7 The Restaurant Plaza Athénée
8 Brasserie Zimmer

Take away the Eiffel Tower, and what is Paris but food? Vainglorious, diet-defying, butter-rich, goose-slaying food. If your goal while in town is to spoil yourself at one of the city's best restaurants, stock up on pâté, or learn to make your own, here is a guide to the best *du jour*. START: **Métro to Sèvres Babylone**

**1** ★ **Poliâne.** This legendary bakery is famous for a reason. So brave the lines, fight your way through, and behold the buttery apple tarts! The melt-in-your-mouth croissants! They are joy baked in an oven. The bread is gorgeous, and the pastries deliver calories to your waist the second you see them, but no matter—this is fuel for your day. *8 rue du Cherche Midi, 6th.* ☎ *01-45-48-42-59. www.poliâne. com. Mon–Sat 7:15am–8:15pm. No credit cards. Métro: Sèvres-Babylone.*

An apple pie at Poliâne.

**2** ★ **La Maison de la Vanille.** It's a good 20-minute walk to this place so you may prefer to take a cab, but vanilla fans should make the effort. This shop gets all of its extraordinary collection of vanilla from Réunion Island, and sells it powdered for baking, liquid for custard, or whole for vanilla sugar and other delicacies. This place smells like heaven. ⏲ *20 min. 18 rue du Cardinal Lemoine, 5th.* ☎ *01-43-25-50-95. Mon 10:30am–7:30pm; Tues–Sat 11am–7:30pm. Closed 2 weeks in Aug. No credit cards. Métro: St-Germain-des-Prés.*

**3** ★ **Marché Mouffetard.** From La Maison de la Vanille, it's about a 10-minute walk to this much-photographed market. As authentic French markets go, this is the most beautiful. Its multicolored wares are stacked on symmetrical stalls stretching down a steep, narrow street. Marketers compete for the

most attractive stall, and you are the beneficiary of their work. Fresh baguettes, croissants, countless cheeses, sausage, fresh-roasted chicken, farm-fresh eggs . . . all are here in abundance. On a nice day, I like to pick up the makings of a picnic lunch here, and then walk over to the Jardin des Plantes (about a 10–15 min. walk) and stretch out on the grass. ⏲ *45 min. The southern end of rue Mouffetard, 5th. Open most weekday & Sat mornings. Métro: Cardinal Lemoine or Censier Daubenton.*

**4** **E Dehillerin.** Stock up on the latest French kitchen equipment at this foodie favorite. This functional warehouse shop is all business when it comes to cooking. It has been supplying fabulous knives and whisks to great chefs for more than a century. The pots and pans may not be cheap, but a Dehillerin sauté pan is forever. *18 rue Coquillière, 1st.* ☎ *01-42-36-53-13. Métro: Les Halles.*

**⑤ ★★★ Ecole Ritz Escoffier.** If you've booked ahead (and if you're a dedicated chef-wannabe, you have), head here for your own cooking class. Deep inside the world-famous Ritz hotel, this cooking school is one of the most respected in the city. It offers a range of classes and demonstrations for cooking fans of all levels. Students learn from talented chefs who take the time to explain everything patiently. (Classes are taught in French and translated into English.) Topics range from bisque-making to chocolate to foie gras. ⏲ *2½–4 hr. 38 rue Cambon, 1st.* ☎ *01-43-16-30-50. www.ritz.com. Book well in advance, as the most interesting classes fill up quickly. Demonstrations 46€, Mon 3–5:30pm; half-day class Sat morning & afternoon from 125€; 3-day courses (summer only) 530€. Métro: Opéra.*

*Parisian markets are a wonderful place to assemble a picnic.*

*A display of wire whisks at E Dehillerin.*

**⑥ Lavinia.** There is no shortage of wine stores in Paris, and somehow all of them manage to be more interesting than wine stores back home. This is one of the largest in Europe, spread over three large stories near place de la Madeleine. Stock up on excellent French wines, or spend some time in the tasting bar or lunch-only restaurant. *3–5 bd. de la Madeleine, 1st.* ☎ *01-42-97-20-20. Métro: Madeleine.*

**⑦ ★★★The Restaurant Plaza Athénée.** Finally, book yourself (months in advance) for a late dinner here. A quick stop at your hotel to dress up, and you're ready to throw yourself into the gastronomical embrace of Alain Ducasse, France's most acclaimed chef. *See p 112.*

**⑧ Brasserie Zimmer.** If Athénée is a bit challenging for your credit card or your patience for rich cuisine, try this friendly, relaxed brasserie for excellent traditional French cuisine at moderate prices. *See p 107.*

# Hemingway's Paris

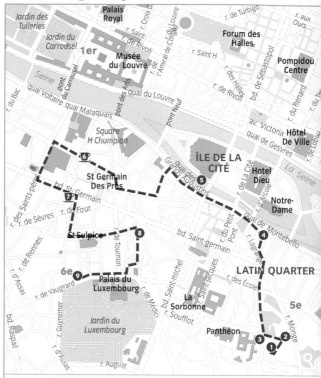

1. Marché Mouffetard
2. Ernest and Hadley's Apartment
3. Hemingway's First Apartment
4. Shakespeare & Company
5. Booksellers along the quai des Grands Augustins
6. Café Pré aux Clercs
7. Les Deux Magots
8. Shakespeare & Company's Original Site
9. Hemingway's Last Apartment

For fans of Papa Hemingway, a trip to Paris is a pilgrimage. This is where Hemingway honed his craft, bullied F. Scott Fitzgerald, and charmed Gertrude Stein. Here he married more than once and had countless mistresses, not the least of which was Paris herself. Oh sure, he cheated on her with Cuba and Spain, but we all know he loved her *really*. This tour follows his spectacular rise and charts the beginning of his fall. START: **Métro to Censier Daubenton**

A vegetable stand at Marché Mouffetard.

**❶ ★ Marché Mouffetard.** At the beginning of his memoir, *A Moveable Feast*, Hemingway describes spending time on rue Mouffetard's "wonderful narrow crowded market street." That description still fits—it's narrow, crowded, and wonderfully Parisian. See p 34, bullet **❸**.

**❷ Ernest & Hadley's Apartment.** Several blocks up rue Mouffetard, rue du Cardinal-Lemoine branches off to the right. A few houses down, on the fourth floor of no. 74, a 22-year-old Hemingway and his wife Hadley rented their first

Parisian apartment together. This was not Hem's first home in Paris, though—that was around the corner on rue Descartes. (See the next stop.) *74 rue du Cardinal-Lemoine, 5th.*

**❸ Hemingway's First Apartment.** When he first moved to Paris as a writer for the *Toronto Star* newspaper, Hemingway took a grimy, cheap room on the top floor of a hotel on rue Descartes. The small wall plaque wrongly states that he lived here for 4 years— he was actually here for 1. *39 rue Descartes, 5th.*

**❹ ★ Shakespeare & Company.** Walk toward the river for about 15 minutes, first on rue Descartes through place Maubert, then down rue F. Sauton, and then take a sharp left onto rue de la

A photo of Hemingway taken in 1930.

Bucherie to reach Paris's best expat bookstore. In the 1920s it was at 11 rue de l'Odéon, and it was at that location that Hemingway broke a vase when he read a bad review, Henry Miller used to "borrow" books and never bring them back, and *Ulysses* was first published. The current location is still a favorite of writers for its eccentric attitude and wonderful selection of books. ⏱ ½–1 hr. *37 rue de la Bucherie, 5th.* ☎ *01-43-26-96-50. Daily noon–midnight. Métro: St-Michel.*

**⑤ Booksellers along Quai des Grands Augustins.** Hemingway frequently shopped here among the secondhand book peddlers along the edge of the Seine. Now, as then, their collections are bewilderingly eclectic—like a flea market for books. The last time I was here I saw the complete Harry Potter collection, in English, next to a book of erotica. ⏱ ½–1 hr. *Quai des Grands Augustins.*

**⑥ Café Pré aux Clercs.** Next you'll come to a series of cafes where you can take a well-deserved rest, as Hem surely would, over a whiskey or a glass of the house red. The first cafe is this charming one

*A used-book stall along the Seine.*

reached by walking down rue des Grands Augustins. (No. 7 was once Pablo Picasso's studio.) Turn onto rue St-Andre des Arts, and then up rue de Seine and left on to antiques shop–lined rue Jacob, which brings you to rue Bonaparte and this cafe. It was one of Hem's early haunts, a short walk from the Hotel d'Angleterre, where he slept (in room no.14) on his first night in Paris. *30 rue Bonaparte, 6th.* ☎ *01-43-54-41-73. $$–$$$*

*Shakespeare & Company is still a popular expat hangout.*

# The 1920s—Americans in Paris

The so-called Lost Generation, led by American expatriates Gertrude Stein and Alice B. Toklas, topped the list of celebrities who "occupied" Paris after World War I. Paris attracted the *litérateur, bon viveur,* and drifter, including writers Henry Miller, Ernest Hemingway, and F. Scott Fitzgerald, and composer Cole Porter.

With the collapse of Wall Street, many Americans returned home. But not hard-core artists like Henry Miller, who wandered around smoking Gauloises when not writing *Tropic of Cancer.* But even such die-hards as Miller eventually realized that 1930s Paris was collapsing as war clouds loomed. Gertrude and Alice remained in France, and are buried together in the Cimetière du Père-Lachaise (p 95, bullet 13).

**7** ★★ **Les de Deux Magots.** Loop down noisy rue des Saints Peres to the more sophisticated hustle of boulevard St-Germain, and soon you'll see the glass front of this cafe, which has gotten more mileage out of the gay '20s than any flapper ever could have. This was the preeminent hangout of the arty expat crowd, where Hemingway charmed the girls, picked fights with the critics, and hassled tourists. The feel today is admittedly touristy, and the food is just adequate (and a bit pricey), but it's still a good place to have a coffee and wonder what he'd think of it all now. *6 place St-Germain-des Prés, 6th.* ☎ 10-45-48-55-25. $$–$$$

**8** **Shakespeare & Company's Original Site.** You can get in a bit of shopping at the many posh boutiques and little jewelry stores on rue St-Sulpice before turning right onto rue de l'Odéon and passing a plaque marking the site of the original Shakespeare & Company bookstore. *11 rue de l'Odéon.*

**9** **Hemingway's Last Apartment.** After turning down rue de Vaugirard and walking past the French Senate, look for this narrow lane near the Jardins du Luxembourg. The impressive building at no. 6 was Ernest Hemingway's last Paris apartment. My, how the fallen became mighty. From the look of its medallions, sphinxes, and heavy gates, you might get the idea that he'd written a successful novel *(The Sun also Rises)* and left poor Hadley for somebody richer (Pauline Pfeiffer). And so he had. Here he reached the summit of his success, and his descent into alcoholism began. *6 rue Férou.*

*Les Deux Magots, with statues of the namesake magistrates on the wall.*

# Paris with Kids

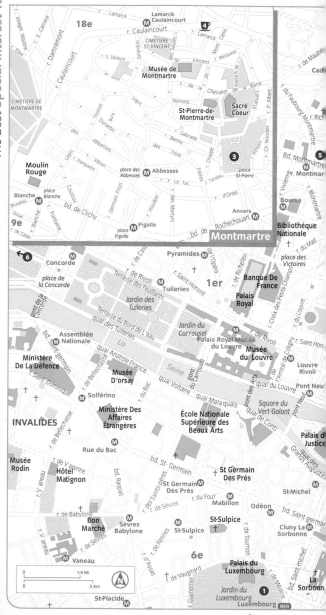

r. Joseph de Maistre
r. Carrière
r. E. Carrière
r. Etex
r. Damrémont
r. Caulaincourt
Lamarck
Lamarck
Caulaincourt
**18e**
r. Caulaincourt
r. Lamarck
Mont Cenis
CIMETIÈRE ST-VINCENT
S. Dereure
r. St. Vincent
r. Becquerel
**4**
r. de Maube
Cad
r. du Faubourg Montmartre
r. Rich
CIMETIÈRE DE MONTMARTRE
Grandon
av. Junot
**Musée de Montmartre**
r. de la Chevalier
de la Barre
Théroine
r. Lepic
Norvins
**St-Pierre-de-Montmartre**
**Sacré Coeur**
r. Albert
r. P. Albert
Bd. Montmartre
**5**
r. Durantin
r. Abbesses
r. Gabrielle
r. Berthe
r. Chappe
Chappe
Rolland
r. Ch. Nodier
Cr. Vivienne
r. Montmartre
**Moulin Rouge**
r. Lepic
r. Planquette
r. Véron
place des Abbesses
**Abbesses**
des
Trois
Frères
Tardieu
Le Tac
place St-Pierre
**3**
r. Montmar
**Blanche**
place Blanche
bd. de Clichy
r. Germain Pilon
r. Houdon
des Martyrs
d'Orsel
**Bourse**
r. Coustou
r. Bruxelles
r. Fontaine
**Blanche**
r. Douai
r. de Calais
place Pigalle
**Pigalle**
bd. de Rochechouart
**Anvers**
**Bibliothèque Nationale**
r. du Mail
**9e**
**Montmartre**
**6**
place des Victoires
**Concorde**
r. de Castl
**Pyramides**
r. de Richelieu
r. de l'Opéra
Banque De France
place de la Concorde
Terrasse des Feuillants
r. de Rivoli
r. St-Honoré
**Tuileries**
**1er**
r. de Richelieu
**Palais Royal**
r. Croix des Petits Champs
r. du Louvre
Jardin des Tuileries
Terrasse du Bord de L'eau
Jardin du Carrousel
**Palais Royal Musée du Louvre**
r. de Rivoli
r. Saint Hon
**Assemblée Nationale**
bd. st. germain
quai des Tuileries
**Musée du Louvre**
r. de l'Amiral de Coligny
**Louvre Rivoli**
**Ministère De La Défense**
La
quai Anatole France
**Musée D'orsay**
Seine
Pont du Carrousel
quai du Louvre
**Pont Neu**
r. Saint-Dominique
r. de Bellechasse
r. du Bac
quai Voltaire
quai Malaquais
pont des Arts
**Square du Vert-Galant**
quai de Conti
**Solférino**
**École Nationale Supérieure des Beaux Arts**
**INVALIDES**
r. de Bellechasse
**Ministère Des Affaires Étrangères**
**Palais de Justice**
quai des Grands Augustins
**Musée Rodin**
r. de Varenne
**Rue du Bac**
bd. St. Germain
**St Germain Des Prés**
**Hôtel Matignon**
r. du Bac
bd. Raspail
**St-Michel**
r. V aneau
**St Germain Des Prés**
r. du Four
r. Saint germain
**Bon Marché**
**Sèvres Babylone**
r. de Babylone
des Saints-pères
**Mabillon**
**Odéon**
bd. Saint germain
r. de Sèvres
**St-Sulpice**
**Cluny La Sorbonne**
r. de Rennes
r. de Tournon
**Vaneau**
r. de Sèvres
**St-Sulpice**
r. d'Assas
**6e**
r. de Vaugirard
r. Guynemer
**Palais du Luxembourg**
r. de Médicis
**La Sorbonn**
bd. Saint-michel
0       1/4 Mi
0       .5 Km
N
**St-Placide**
r. de Vaugirard
**Jardin du Luxembourg**
**Luxembourg** RER
**1**

**1** Jardins du Luxembourg

**2** Musée National d'Histoire Naturelle

**3** Funicular to Sacré Coeur

**4** Francis Labutte

**5** Grévin

**6** Jardin d'Acclimatation

I can say this without hesitation: I have never seen a happy-looking child under 12 in the Louvre. Think twice before you drag one there. Most kid-approved attractions are outdoors, which means you're dangerously reliant on good weather, but if you get a little sun there's plenty to keep them smiling. If all else fails, rush them off for a day at Disneyland Paris. (See the tour on p 156.) START: **Métro to Odéon**

*Kids can rent toy sailboats at the Jardins du Luxembourg.*

### ❶ Jardins du Luxembourg.

Kids can run amok in these elegant gardens, which are done in classic French style, with urns and statuary and trees planted in patterns. Statues peek out everywhere as children sail toy boats on the ponds, ride the ponies, or catch a puppet show, if you get lucky with timing. Kids can also watch the locals play *boules* (lawn bowling), but are unlikely to be invited to join in. Don't miss the ornate, evocative Fountaines de Medicis, in the northeast corner of the park. 🕐 *1 hr. Métro: Odéon.*

### ❷ Musée National d'Histoire Naturelle.

The giant whale skeleton hanging just inside the front door of this natural history museum lets you know right off the bat that the kids are going to be fine here. Beyond those bones are more skeletons of dinosaurs and mastodons, and galleries filled with sparkling minerals and rare plants. There's even a menagerie with small animals in simulated natural habitats. A good place to linger if the weather turns gray. 🕐 *1½ hr. 57 rue Cuvier, 5th.* ☎ *01-40-79-30-00. www.mnhn.fr. Admission 7€, 5€ for kids under 16. Wed–Mon 10am–5pm. Métro: Jussieu or Gare d'Austerlitz.*

### ❸ ★ Funicular to Sacré Coeur.

Take the Métro to Abbesses, then follow the signs to the funicular. The ride will thrill the kids with its steep climb and great views. At the top of the hill are telescopes for

*A dinosaur at the Musée National d'Histoire Naturelle.*

*A boy ponders French philosopher Jean-Paul Sartre's wax sculpture.*

closer views of the city far below you. ⏱ *1 hr. Place St Pierre. The funicular takes Métro tickets.*

**4** ★ **Francis Labutte.** Skip the expensive, tourist-packed cafes near the Sacré Coeur and head down the back of the hill to this charming place. The dining room is colorful, the heated terrace (covered in winter) is abuzz, and the noise means nobody will tell the little ones to hush. Try the *croques monsieurs* (grilled ham-and-cheese sandwiches) and vegetarian tarts. *122 rue Caulaincourt, 18th.* ☎ *10-42-23-58-26. $$*

**5** **Grévin.** If the weather is bad, make this your last stop of the day. If it's good, skip this stop and go on to the next one. At this waxworks museum, kids will enjoy wandering among stars—both American (Madonna) and international (soccer star Zinédine Zidane). Among the 300 wax figures you'll find heads of state, artists, writers, and historical figures—at times the museum even

verges on educational. ⏱ *1 hr. 10 bd. Montmartre, 9th.* ☎ *02-47-70-95-05. www.musee-grevin.com. Admission 16€, 9€ for kids 6–14, free for kids under 6. Mon–Fri 10am–6:30pm; Sat–Sun 10am–7pm. Métro: Grands-Boulevards.*

**6** ★★ **Jardin d'Acclimatation.** Let the kids while away the rest of a sunny afternoon here. You can start with a ride on a green-and-yellow narrow-gauge train from porte Maillot to the entrance (every 30 min. Wed and Sat–Sun). Along the way there's a house of mirrors, an archery range, miniature golf, a small (and vaguely worrying) zoo, a bowling alley, a puppet theater, playgrounds, kid-size rides, shooting galleries, and food stalls. Kids can ride ponies and paddle about in boats—they can even drive little cars. Bear in mind that it's only for little ones; teenagers will hate it. ⏱ *2–3 hr. In the Bois de Boulogne, 16th.* ☎ *01-40-67-90-82. www.jardin dacclimatation.fr. Admission 2.50€, free for kids under 4. Train rides 1.25€ one-way. June–Sept daily 10am–7pm; Oct–May daily 10am–6pm. Métro: Sablons or Porte Maillot.*

# Romantic Paris

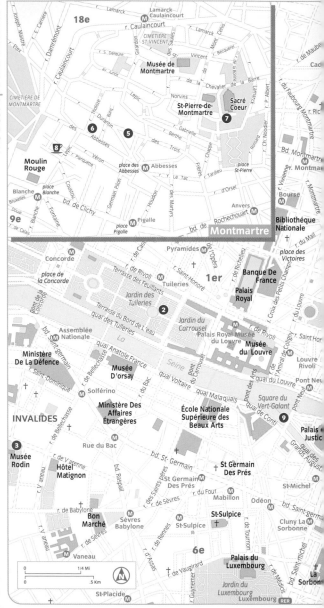

1. Pont Royal
2. Jardin des Tuileries
3. Musée Rodin
4. Viaduc des Arts
5. Montmartre
6. rue Tholoze
7. Sacré Coeur
8. Café des Deux Moulins
9. Bateaux mouches

**W**hen it comes to romance and Paris, all the clichés are true. Its pastel-pink sunsets, creamy buildings, glorious art, and relaxing cafes all suffuse the city with lazy loving languor. It's hard to go wrong here, but, for what it's worth, these are my favorite places for a little romance. START: **Métro to Palais Royal**

A couple enjoying the Jardin des Tuileries.

**①** ★★★ **Kissing on the Nont Royal.** Actually, any of the bridges over the Seine will do. But I like this one because it has benches in the middle where you can sit, take in the view down the lacy lines of the river, and steal a kiss or two. ⏲ 15 min. Métro: Palais Royal.

**②** ★ **Wandering in the Jardin des Tuileries.** With its wide clay paths and tall, feathery trees, this park gets better the farther you get from the Louvre. I always wander toward the second pond, where it's less crowded, and find a seat under the trees. For more information, check out "Jardin des Tuileries" on p 90. ⏲ 1 hr. Métro: Palais Royal or Louvre Rivoli.

**③** ★★ **Musée Rodin.** This peaceful museum, housed in the building that was once Rodin's studio, can't help but inspire thoughts of romance. *The Thinker* ponders in the courtyard while the lovers in *Le Baiser* are locked in a permanent embrace inside. ⏲ 1 hr. Hôtel Biron, 77 rue de Varenne, 7th. ☎ 01-44-18-61-10. www.musee-rodin.fr. *Rarely crowded, so a good option when things are busy at the Louvre. Admission 5€, free for kids under 17. Apr–Sept Tues–Sun 9:30am–5:45pm; Oct–Mar Tues–Sun 9:30am–4:45pm. Métro: Varenne.*

**④** ★★ **Viaduc des Arts.** What does Paris do with an unused railway viaduct just behind the Opéra Bastille? Turn it into something hopelessly romantic, of course. This old rail line is now a row of posh boutiques surrounded by the lush green promenade Plantée, cleverly designed with myriad little paths

Detail of Rodin's Le Baiser (The Kiss), sculpted in 1886.

*A romantic twilight cruise along the Seine.*

playing peekaboo in and out of the greenery. Made for love? Oh, yes. ⏱ *1 hr. Av. Daumesnil, 12th. Métro: Gare de Lyon.*

**5** ★★★ **Montmartre.** This is widely considered the most romantic neighborhood in Paris, and for good reasons. Its adorable cafes, stair-step streets, windmills, and beauty make it irresistible. Spending an afternoon here should rekindle passion in just about any heart. See the Montmartre tour on p 68. ⏱ *2 hr. Métro: Abbesses.*

**6** ★★ **Rue Tholoze.** This little Montmartre lane is the city's steepest street, and one of its most charming. Start at rue Abbesses and stroll up toward rue Lepic. On either side, the 18th-century houses lean to keep their balance as one of Montmartre's two windmills sits immobile at the top. A perfect photo opportunity. ⏱ *15 min. Métro: Abbesses.*

**7** ★★★ **The View from the Sacré Coeur.** If you turn right on rue Lepic, then take the winding lanes up past place du Tertre, you'll soon see the creamy white basilica of the Sacré Coeur. The church itself is attraction enough, but stand at the viewing spot in front for the real payoff: There is all of Paris spread out before you, like a pale, delicate blanket. ⏱ *1 hr. Place St-Pierre, 18th.* ☎ *01-53-41-89-00. www.paris. org/Monuments. Free admission to basilica; dome & crypt 5€. Daily 6am–11pm. Métro: Abbesses.*

**8** ★★★ **Café des Deux Moulins.** Head back down rue Lepic for a well-deserved pause. This sweet retro cafe starred in the romantic French film *Amelie*, and draws in nostalgic lovers every day. *15 rue Lepic, 18th.* ☎ *01-42-54-90-50. Métro: Abbesses. $–$$*

**9** ★★★ **Bateaux Mouches.** These old tour boats don't seem romantic at first glance, but they can melt your heart, particularly at night. Their motors putt-putt along the Seine past the city's beautiful buildings, all aglow—the whole experience is simply unforgettable. *In summer, the bateaux agency at the pont de l'Alma (Bateaux Mouches) has boats every 30 min. until 9pm (7€), the one at the pont Neuf (Bateaux Vedettes du Pont Neuf) until 10:30pm (9€) & the one by the Tour Eiffel (Bateaux Parisiens) until 11pm (9€).*

# On the Trail of *The Da Vinci Code*

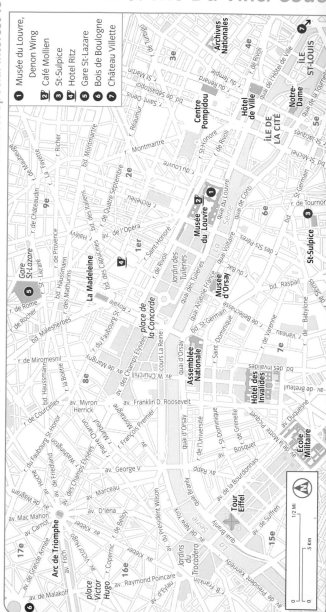

1 Musée du Louvre, Denon Wing
2' Café Mollien
3 St-Sulpice
4 Hotel Ritz
5 Gare St-Lazare
6 Bois de Boulogne
7 Château Villette

**D**espite an obscure plot about the search for the "lost sacred feminine," Knights Templar, and academicians running amok, Dan Brown's page-turner is a literary sales phenomenon and a boon for Paris. Parisians laugh at Brown's geography and scoff at his characters' ability to leap out of the Louvre and arrive miles away within minutes, but it's still entertaining to follow the path they take as they desperately attempt to unravel a complex mystery. START: **Métro to Palais Royal–Musée du Louvre**

**1** ★★★ **Musée du Louvre, Denon Wing.** In Paris to receive an award for his work, art professor Robert Langdon gets tangled up in a murder mystery after art expert Jacques Saunière's body is found here, not far from two paintings by Leonardo da Vinci. Near the body, the police find a coded message: a series of clues to the location of the Holy Grail. Most of da Vinci's paintings are at the end of Denon's Long Gallery, in Room 13—you may have to look around, though, as this section is being renovated. In the book, da Vinci's *Madonna of the Rocks* is used by Langdon's cohort, Sophie Neveu, as blackmail when police attempt to arrest the two. Farther down the corridor hangs the *Mona Lisa,* which Langdon theorizes was meant to be a painting of both a man *and* a woman. *See p 13, bullet* **1**.

**2** ★★ **Café Mollien.** You're sure to work up an appetite trekking through the Louvre. My favorite Louvre cafe is Café Mollien, for its terrace and fresh sandwiches. *$*

**3** ★★ **St-Sulpice.** A mysterious albino monk visits St-Sulpice late at night to search for clues to the location of the Grail. Near the middle of the nave on the right side, you can locate one end of the Rose Line—a narrow brass strip marking the original zero-longitude line, which passed through Paris before it was relocated to Greenwich, England. The monk uses the Rose Line as a guide in his search for clues. The organ described in the book—one of the world's largest—is in a back chapel. While you're here, depart from the book for a moment to admire the Delacroix frescoes in the

*The Denon Wing of the Louvre.*

*The monk Silas follows a fake clue to this obelisk in St-Sulpice church.*

Chapelle des Anges, the first chapel on your right as you enter. ⏰ *45 min. Place St-Sulpice, 6th.* ☎ *01-46-33-21-78. Free admission. Daily 8:30am–8pm. Métro: St-Sulpice.*

**4** ★★ **Hotel Ritz.** In the book's first scene, Robert Langdon receives a phone call from the police in his elegant room at this luxury hotel. If you can't afford a room here (400€ nightly; clearly Mr. Langdon was here on expenses, as that's well out of most university professors' league), you can probably handle a cocktail in its historic Hemingway Bar. *15 place Vendome, 1st.* ☎ *01-43-16-30-30. Métro: Opéra. $$$*

**5** **Gare St-Lazare.** After escaping from the police, Neveu and Langdon leave the Louvre in her car, heading first to the rue de Rivoli and then down the Champs-Elysées to the Arc de Triomphe, where she turns sharply down boulevard Malesherbes to this train station. (You may recognize it if you're a Monet fan—he painted it in 1877.) Here Neveu purchases train tickets to Lille as a decoy. You can cunningly convince a Parisian cab driver to take the same route. *108 rue St-Lazare, 8th. Métro: Gare St-Lazare.*

**6** ★★★ **Bois de Boulogne.** Later, Neveu and Langdon speed through the Bois de Boulogne's allée de Longchamp to the Depository Bank of Zurich, where the messages from Saunière indicate they'll find more clues. In the book the fictitious bank was near the Roland Garros tennis stadium, in the park. With its wide paths, lakes, and playgrounds, the Bois is popular during the day with joggers, strollers, and families. As the novel indicates, the park is much different at night, when prostitutes waiting for customers line sections of allée de Longchamp. If you decide not to make the trek to Château Villette (the next stop), you could easily spend the rest of the day here—see the "Exploring Bois de Boulogne" tour on p 96. ⏰ *20 min. Main entrance at bottom of av. Foch, 16th. Métro: Porte Maillot, Porte Dauphine, or Porte d'Auteuil.*

**7** ★★ **Château Villette.** Pursued by French authorities, Neveu and Langdon drive out of town to the 17th-century Château Villette, owned by Langdon's friend, British art historian Sir Leigh Teabing. The building is real, but you'll need a car to get here—it's about 30 minutes outside of Paris, near Versailles. Even the most dedicated fans might not want to bother, given that the château is privately owned and not regularly open to the public. Wealthy *Da Vinci Code* fans can spend 6,500€ a week per person for a stay here along with a "Da Vinci Code" tour. You can also take a 2-hour tour for 55€ per person for groups of 15 people, or 45€ per person for groups of 25 or more. To book a weeklong stay, e-mail villette@frenchvacation.com; for the shorter tours, e-mail villette@chateauxcountry.com. For spring and fall culinary and photography classes at the château, visit www.thetasteoffrance.com. ☎ *01-53-67-74-00.* ●

# The Latin Quarter

1 Place St-Michel
2 rue du Chat-qui-Pêche
3 Eglise St-Séverin
4 Eglise St-Julien-le-Pauvre
5 Musée National du Moyen
　Age-Thermes de Cluny
6 La Sorbonne
7 Eglise de la Sorbonne
8 Le Panthéon
9 Les Papilles

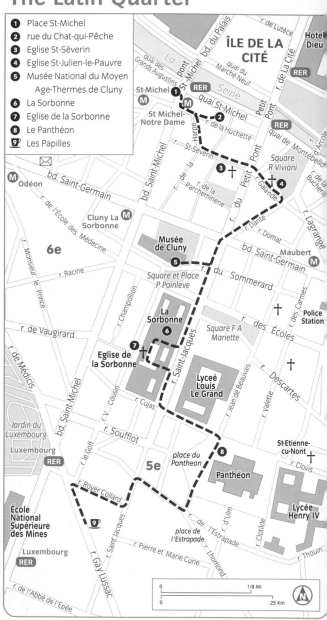

In the 1920s this was the heart of Paris's cafe society. You'll still find plenty of cafes, plus universities and shops, all constantly buzzing with activity. It's one of my favorite places in Paris. **START: Métro to St-Michel**

*A busy cafe on place St-Michel.*

**❶ Place St-Michel.** An elaborate 1860 statue of Saint Michael slaying a dragon presides over this bustling cafe- and shop-lined square, where skirmishes between occupying Germans and French Resistance fighters once took place. This is the beginning of busy boulevard St-Michel, which was trendy long ago, but is now a disappointing line of fast-food chains and down-market stores.

**❷ Rue du Chat-qui-Pêche.** Turn down rue de la Huchette, bypassing its endless kabob and pizza joints to reach this street which, for what it's worth, claims to be the narrowest in Paris. It is tiny indeed, and also dirty and grim. Its name—"Street of the Cat Who Fishes"—rises above the garbage,

however. There are plenty of local tales about the history of the name, but nobody knows for sure. Still, the sign makes a great photo.

**❸ Eglise St-Séverin.** Head back toward place St-Michel and turn left on rue de la Harpe, which leads to rue St-Séverin and this charming medieval church, built in the early 13th century and reconstructed in the 15th. Don't miss the whimsical gargoyles and monsters projecting from the roof. Inside, I like to linger over the rare Rouault etchings from the 1920s. ⏱ *30 min. 1 rue des Pretres-St Severin, 5th.* ☎ *01-42-34-93-50. Mon–Sat 11am–7:30pm; Sun 9am–10:30pm.*

**❹ Eglise St-Julien-le-Pauvre.** Take rue St-Séverin to rue Galande, and after snapping a picture of its quaint old houses, find this medieval church, which dates, at least in part, to 1170. Note the unusual

*The Latin Quarter at night, with St-Séverin church in the background.*

*The Cluny museum building was once the mansion of a rich 15th-century abbot.*

capitals covered in carved vines and leaves. The garden has one of my favorite views of Notre-Dame. ⏱ *20 min. Rue St-Julien-le-Pauvre, 5th.* ☎ *01-43-54-52-16. Mon–Sat 9:30am–noon, 3–6:30pm. Métro: La Sorbonne.*

**⑤ ★ Musée National du Moyen Age–Thermes de Cluny.** With one of the world's strongest collections of medieval art, this small, manageable museum is a gem. Most of the people in line ahead of you are here to see its wallowing-in-romance–style *Lady and the Unicorn* tapestries. But there's much more here than long-haired maidens and mythical creatures: This 15th-century Gothic building sits atop 2nd-century baths. The Gallo-Roman pools are in excellent shape—the frigidarium (cold bath) and tepidarium (warm bath) can still be clearly seen (though you can no longer take a dip). ⏱ *1 hr. 6 place Paul-Painlevé, 5th.* ☎ *01-53-73-78-00. www. musee moyenage.fr. Admission*

*5.50€. Wed–Mon 9:15am–5:45pm. Métro: Cluny–La Sorbonne.*

**⑥ ★ La Sorbonne.** France's most famous university, dating back some 700 years, has all the venerable buildings and confident, beret-wearing students you might imagine. Teachers here have included Thomas Aquinas, and the alumni association counts Dante, Calvin, and Longfellow among its past members. This is a sprawling place, and only the courtyard and galleries are open to the public when school is in session—follow the crowds and the scarce signs to get a peek. ⏱ *30 min. 12 rue de la Sorbonne, 5th.* ☎ *01-44-07-80-00. www.sorbonne.fr. Métro: Cluny–La Sorbonne.*

**⑦ ★ Eglise de la Sorbonne.** On the grounds of the Sorbonne, this 17th-century church holds the elaborate tomb of Cardinal Richelieu (1585–1642). Richelieu was a staunch defender of the monarchy's power and did much to unify the French state. The extraordinary statue at its feet is poignantly named *Learning in Tears;* the figure mourning at the

*Detail of the* Lady and the Unicorn *tapestries.*

*Students at La Sorbonne.*

cardinal's feet represents science, and the one supporting him represents religion. ⏱ *30 min. Rue de la Sorbonne, 5th.*

**8** ★★ **Le Panthéon.** This magnificent building was built by Louis XV as a tribute to Saint Geneviève. (Construction began in 1758.) Since the Revolution, however, it's been used to honor more earthly heroes. Here are France's great dead, including Voltaire, Rousseau, Emile Zola, and Victor Hugo. Recent additions include Marie Curie, whose remains were moved here in 1995, and Alexandre Dumas, who arrived in 2002. Appropriately, there's a Foucault's pendulum here—the famous device, which proved that the earth rotates on an axis, was said to hang from "the eye of God." Although the pendulum appears to swing, it's not moving—the earth is. ⏱ *1 hr. Place du Panthéon, 5th.* ☎ *01-44-32-18-00. Admission 7€. Daily 10am–7:15pm. Métro: Cardinal Lemoine. RER: Luxembourg.*

**9** **Les Papilles.** Dying for a break? This is just the place. The owners of this sweet, Provençal-style cafe are dedicated to Southern French food and adventurous wine. The menu changes with the seasons, and the wines change with the owners' moods. If they're available, try the excellent stewed chicken or the hearty cassoulet. *30 rue Gay-Lussac, 5th.* ☎ *01-43-25-20-79. RER: Luxembourg. $$*

*Interior of the Panthéon.*

# St-Germain-des-Prés

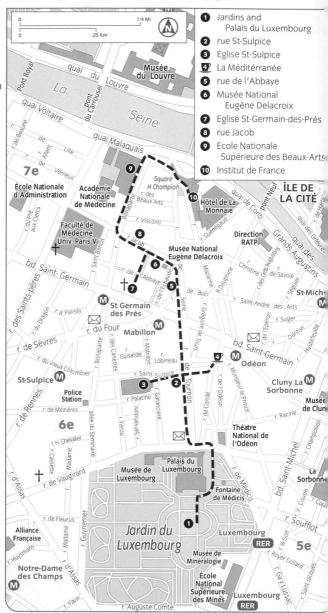

1 Jardins and Palais du Luxembourg

2 rue St-Sulpice

3 Eglise St-Sulpice

4 La Méditérranée

5 rue de l'Abbaye

6 Musée National Eugène Delacroix

7 Eglise St-Germain-des-Prés

8 rue Jacob

9 Ecole Nationale Supérieure des Beaux-Arts

10 Institut de France

This was the place to be in the 1920s. Here the literati met the glitterati and *tout* Paris marveled at the ensuing explosion of creativity and alcoholism. On these streets Sartre fumed, while Hemingway and Fitzgerald drank and quarreled. Today the bookshops have been replaced by designer boutiques, but it's still the place to go for a night on the town. START: **Métro to Luxembourg**

*Relaxing in the Jardins du Luxembourg.*

**1** ★★★ **kids** **Jardins & Palais du Luxembourg.** There's a certain justice in the fact that this former palace, built between 1615 and 1627 for the widow of Henry IV, is now home to the democratically elected French Senate. As lovely as the Italianate building is, though you're really here for the gardens. The picturesque paths of the Jardins du Luxembourg have always been a favorite of artists, although children, students from the nearby Sorbonne, and tourists are more common than painters nowadays. Hemingway claimed to have survived a winter by stealing pigeons from here for his supper, and Gertrude Stein used to cross the gardens on her way to sit for Picasso. The classic formal gardens are done in the French tradition: well groomed and symmetrically designed. And there are statues everywhere—more than 80 of them vie for your attention. Every time I visit the vast sculpted grounds I discover a new pond in which children float paper boats, or a statue I never noticed before—a long-haired French queen, a tiny Statue of Liberty, a huge Cyclops. It's fanciful and delightful; you could spend hours here and never find all of its secrets. 🕐 *1 hr. Métro: Odéon.*

**2** **Rue St-Sulpice.** Turn down any street on the river side of the gardens and walk a few blocks to rue St-Sulpice. Welcome to shopping heaven (or window-shopping purgatory, if you're like me). This is Paris's answer to New York's Fifth

*Christian Lacroix's shop window.*

Avenue or London's Bond Street. All the usual designer suspects are here for your inspection—agnès b., Christian Lacroix, Catherine Memmi, perfumer Annick Goutal, and friends. If you want to stock up for a picnic, pop down rue du Cherche-Midi to Poilâne bakery for some of the city's best breads and sandwiches to go.

❸ ★★ **Eglise St-Sulpice.** Filled with paintings by Delacroix, including *Jacob's Fight with the Angel*, this was a wonderful, quiet church to wander in until the novel *The Da Vinci Code* was published. St-Sulpice plays a major role in the book, and now it tends to be crowded with readers taking in its gorgeous frescoes. *See p 49, bullet* ❸.

*Detail of some of the painted columns at Eglise St-Germain-des-Prés.*

❹ **La Méditérranée.** A short walk away lies this restaurant filled with murals by 20th-century stage designers Christian Bérard and Marcel Vertés, and paintings by Picasso and Chagall. It was once a haunt of Jackie Kennedy, Picasso, and Cocteau (whose work enlivens the plates and menus). The chef delivers creative interpretations of traditional dishes, including gorgeous fried fish with fresh spinach salad, and an incredible bouillabaisse, thick with seafood. The prix-fixe menu ranges from 25€ to 29€. *2 place de l'Odéon, 6th.* ☎ 01-43-26-02-30. *Métro: Odéon.* $$$

❺ **Rue de l'Abbaye.** St-Germain was built around an old abbey that once towered over this street, although there's virtually nothing left of it today. With houses and churches built of red brick, the street is charming, particularly place Furstenberg—once the abbot's stables, it's now filled with upmarket interior design shops.

❻ ★ **Musée National Eugène Delacroix.** The Romantic painter Eugène Delacroix lived and worked in this lovely house in place Furstenberg from 1857 until his death in 1863. The museum sits on a charming square, with a romantic garden. Most of his major works are in the Louvre, but the collection here is unusually personal, including an early self-portrait and letters and notes to friends like Baudelaire and George Sand. You can also see his work in the Chapelle des Anges in Eglise St-Sulpice (see stop 3 on this tour). ⏱ 1 hr. 6 place Furstenberg, 6th. ☎ 01-44-41-86-50. www. musee-delacroix.fr. Admission 4€. Wed–Mon 9:30am–5pm. Métro: St-Germain-des-Prés.

❼ ★ **Eglise St-Germain-des-Prés.** This exquisite little church is the oldest in Paris, and a rarity in France—only a few buildings this old exist in such complete form. It dates to the 6th century, when a Benedictine abbey was founded here, though little remains from that time. Its aged columns still bear their medieval paint in breathtaking detail. You can visit the tomb of the French philosopher René Descartes (1596–1650) in the second chapel. At one time, the abbey was a pantheon for Merovingian kings. During the restoration of the site of their tombs, Chapelle de St-Symphorien, previously unknown Romanesque paintings were discovered. ⏱ *30 min. 3 place St-Germain-des-Prés, 6th.* ☎ *01-43-25-41-71. Mon–Sat 8am–7:45pm; Sun 9am–8pm. Métro: St-Germain-des-Prés.*

**⑧ Rue Jacob.** This elegant street, with clean lines and classic 19th-century architecture, was once home to such illustrious residents as the writer Colette and the composer Richard Wagner. Today it holds charming bookstores and antiques shops, and is all very posh-bohemian—especially the popular Aux Assassins cabaret (no. 40), with naughty postcards on the walls, singers belting out vaguely dirty songs in French, and tables crowded with titillated members of the bourgeoisie.

**⑨ Ecole Nationale Supérieure des Beaux-Arts.** Turn onto rue Bonaparte and walk toward the river to reach this fine-arts school, where the main attraction is the architecture. The school occupies a 17th-century convent and the 18th-century Hôtel de Chimay. Attending an exhibition (held frequently) will grant you a peek inside, but if none are on, I'm always happy to wander down rue Bonaparte, which is lined with lovely small art galleries. ⏱ *30 min. 14 rue Bonaparte, 6th.* ☎ *01-47-03-52-15. www.ensba.fr. Courtyard Mon–Fri 9am–5pm; exhibitions Tues–Sun 1–7pm. Métro: St-Germain-des-Prés.*

**⑩ Institut de France.** Turn right along the river and you'll see a hard-to-miss elegant domed baroque building, home to five

sub-governmental agencies all lumped together as the rather ominously named *l'Institut.* Here the Académie Française zealously (some would say too zealously) guards the purity of the French language from "Franglais" encroachment (Jacques Cousteau was once a member), while other, lesser known agencies (Sciences, Inscriptions et Belles Lettres, Beaux-Arts, and Sciences Morales et Politiques) do . . . whatever it is they do. The brave can arrange for a guided tour (available in English). You can also peek into a few of the buildings on your own, but most are closed to the public—perhaps not surprisingly, considering that academy members are known as "the Immortals." Good Lord. ⏱ *15 min. 23 quai de Conti, 6th.* ☎ *01-44-41-44-41. Admission 3.50€. Guided tours Sat–Sun (call ahead for times). Métro: St-Germain-des-Prés.*

*Brasserie Lipp (151 bd. St-Germain) is a Left Bank institution and former Hemingway haunt.*

# The Islands

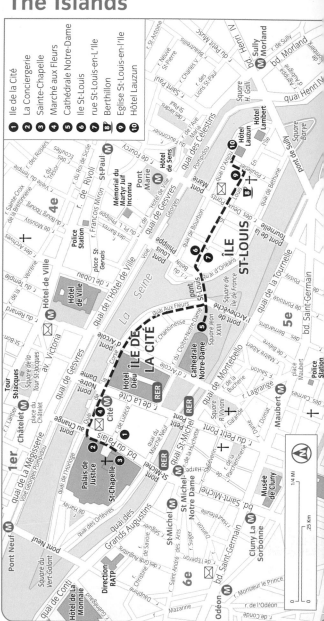

**B**efore I first visited Paris, I could never picture the islands that feature so heavily in the city's history and literature. When I finally saw them, though, it all made sense. The islands in the Seine fit like pieces of a puzzle, each with its own personality, but all unmistakably Parisian. START: **Métro to Cité**

**1 Ile de la Cité.** Paris was founded here on the "Isle of the City" by a tribe of Celts called the Parisii. By medieval times this was a thriving island town. Few have written more movingly about its heyday than Victor Hugo, who invited the reader "to observe the fantastic display of lights against the darkness of that gloomy labyrinth of buildings; cast upon it a ray of moonlight, showing the city in glimmering vagueness, with its towers lifting their great heads from that foggy sea." During the 19th century, most of the residents were moved to the Marais. The best way to reach Ile de la Cité is via the bridge known as pont Neuf. The name means "new bridge"—ironic considering that it's Paris's oldest bridge, dating back to the time of Catherine of Medici in the 16th century. I often linger here to take in the view and watch the crowds around the statue of Henri IV.

**2 ★ La Conciergerie.** This intimidating building, originally a 14th-century fortress, was converted into a prison during the Revolution, and became an object of terror to the public at a time when idle accusations could result in spontaneous executions. Marie Antoinette, Danton, and Robespierre all were held here before being guillotined. Today you can see the cells where they were held, and the rooms where they were tried and condemned. A strange and interesting place. *See p 23.*

**3 ★ Sainte-Chapelle.** Tucked away among the huge Conciergerie and the vast law courts of the Palais de Justice, this tiny church is as hard to find as a diamond in a coal mine, but persevere, because it's a precious place, made almost entirely of dazzling stained glass windows. Unfortunately, it's not undiscovered, and I've found it in the past by following the crowds to a long line waiting to get in. *See p 23, bullet* **3**.

*Pont Neuf, with La Conciergerie in the background.*

*Many of the flowers at Marché aux Fleurs are shipped in from the French Riviera.*

**❹ Marché aux Fleurs.** This vivid flower market is a photo opportunity simply crying out for your camera. It must be one of the most photographed places on earth—and for good reason. On Sunday it's transformed into a bird market. ⏱ *30 min. Place Louis Lépine, quai de la Corse, quai des Fleurs, 4th. Mon–Sat 8am–7:30pm; Sun 8am–7pm. Métro: Cité.*

*Sainte-Chapelle's stained-glass windows are stunning on a sunny day.*

**❺ ★★★ Cathédrale Notre-Dame.** This world-famous cathedral is more beautiful in person than on film. You'll marvel at its lacy golden walls, delicate windows, and sheer beauty. *See p 9, bullet ❼.*

**❻ Ile St-Louis.** The smaller of the Seine's islands has a subtle charm that is hard to categorize. Ile St-Louis has hosted everybody in the French literary world from Racine to Molière at one point or another, although few writers less wealthy than Stephen King could afford an apartment here now—the 17th-century buildings lining its narrow streets are some of the city's most expensive property. It's a lovely place to wander, and so tiny it's almost impossible to get lost.

**❼ Rue St-Louis-en-L'Ile.** I can spend hours strolling this relatively short street, stepping into its boutiques, trying on silk scarves, and practicing my French on the helpful sales assistants. Hôtel Chenizot, at no. 51, has fantastic carved dragons and fauns on its facade. From the end of the street closest to the Ile de la Cité, I've taken great photos of Notre-Dame.

**8 Berthillon.** On Ile St-Louis, even the ice-cream stores are sophisticated. This place proves it, with polite crowds queuing outside for cones to go, and others perched at the tables inside to try the lemon, hazelnut, and mango flavors favored by the locals—it's always chocolate for me. *31 rue St-Louis-en-l'Ile, 4th. Métro: Pont Marie. $*

**9 Eglise St-Louis-en-l'Ile.** This 17th-century church, vastly over-shadowed by its famous neighbor, has your basic baroque architecture with a lovely sunburst above the altar. It might be a bit anti-climactic after seeing Notre-Dame, but it's worth a quick stop. ⏱ *20 min. 19 rue St-Louis-en-l'Ile, 4th.* ☎ *01-46-34-11-60. Tues–Sun 9am–noon, 3–7pm. Métro: Pont Marie.*

**10 ★★ Hôtel Lauzun.** This astonishing place, with fantastic drains in the shapes of sea serpents, was the scene of famously long, hazy hashish parties thrown by Baudelaire and Théophile Gautier. Baudelaire wrote *Les Fleurs Du Mal* while living here, although it's hard to see how he could have been so

*A sea-serpent drainpipe at Hôtel Lauzun.*

depressed living somewhere so pretty. The building takes its name from a former occupant, the duc de Lauzun. He was a favorite of Louis XIV until he asked for the hand of the king's cousin, the duchesse de Montpensier. Louis refused and had Lauzun tossed into the Bastille. Eventually the duchesse convinced Louis to release him, and they married secretly and moved here in 1682. *17 quai d'Anjou. Generally closed to the public, although sometimes there are art exhibits here— check with the tourist office. Métro: Pont Marie.*

*View of Notre-Dame from Ile St-Louis.*

# The Marais

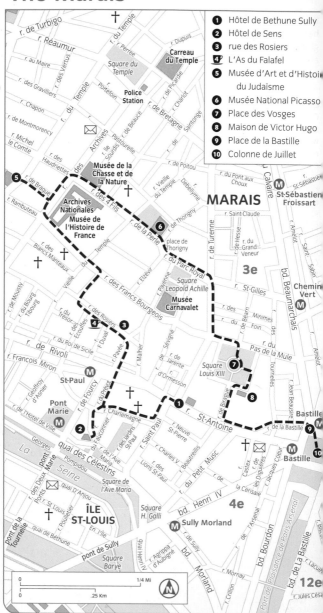

1 Hôtel de Bethune Sully
2 Hôtel de Sens
3 rue des Rosiers
4 L'As du Falafel
5 Musée d'Art et d'Histoir du Judaïsme
6 Musée National Picasso
7 Place des Vosges
8 Maison de Victor Hugo
9 Place de la Bastille
10 Colonne de Juillet

When Ile de la Cité became overcrowded, it was here, to what had been swampland, that the Parisians moved, filling the streets with fashionable mansions called *hôtels*. Over the years it became the center of the city's Jewish community, though today the gay and lesbian community has adopted the area. Its many boutiques and diverse buildings make for excellent shopping and exploring.

START: **Métro to St Paul**

**1 Hôtel de Bethune Sully.** Out of the Métro, turn right on rue St-Antoine. This gracious mansion was restored not long ago and its relief-studded facade dazzles once again, as it was meant to when it was first designed in 1634. Once a private home, it now holds government offices, but there's a bookstore and information center, and guided tours are sometimes available on weekends. The charming garden is always open. ⏱ *20 min. 62 rue St-Antoine. Inquire about tours at the information center. Métro: St-Paul.*

**2 Hôtel de Sens.** Given the leaded windows and fairy-tale turrets, you might not be surprised to find that this 15th-century mansion has a gloriously ornate courtyard in which you can wander at will most afternoons. Once a private home for archbishops and, later, queens, it now holds a library, the Bibliothèque Forney. ⏱ *20 min. 1 rue du Figurier.* ☎ *01-42-78-14-60. Courtyard open Tues–Fri 1:30–8:15pm; Sat 10am–8:15pm. Métro: St-Paul.*

**3 Rue des Rosiers.** Perhaps the most colorful and typical street remaining from the time when this was the city's Jewish quarter, rue des Rosiers (Street of the Rosebushes) meanders among the old buildings with nary a rose to be seen. At some points it's barely wider than two people walking side by side. I'm a regular at the falafel cafes on this street, and often grab a good cheap lunch here.

*The Hôtel de Sens once housed the archbishops of Sens.*

The Marais has a growing gay and lesbian population; an anti-homophobia demonstration is pictured.

**4** ★ **L'As du Falafel.** This tiny cafe is one of my favorite lunch places in Paris, with the best falafel sandwiches (4€) in the city. They don't speak any English here, but they communicate just fine anyway. Unless it's raining, I get mine to go (there's a window for takeout orders), and eat them on a bench in the place des Vosges. (See stop 7 on this tour.) *34 rue des Rosiers, 4th.* ☎ *01-48-87-63-60.* $

**5** ★ **Musée d'Art et d'Histoire du Judaïsme.** This museum was created in 1948 to protect the city's Jewish history after the Holocaust. It's a moving place, with excellent Jewish decorative arts from around Europe—German Hanukkah lamps, a wooden *sukkah* cabin from Austria—and documents related to Jewish history in Europe. There's also a memorial to the Jews who lived in the building in 1939, 13 of whom died in concentration camps. ⏱ *45 min. Hôtel de St-Aignan, 71 rue du Temple, 3rd.* ☎ *01-53-01-86-60.*

www.mahj.org. Mon–Fri 11am–6pm; Sun 10am–6pm. Admission 6.20€. Métro: Rambuteau.

**6** **Musée National Picasso.** Located inside the grand Hôtel Salé, this extraordinary little museum is the result of a tax seizure—when Picasso and his wife died in the early 1970s, the French government took the art from Picasso's family in lieu of $50 million in inheritance taxes. The state did very well in the deal, acquiring 203 paintings and 158 sculptures, including *Man with a Guitar* and studies for *Les Demoiselles d'Avignon,* the work that launched cubism in 1907. A must-see for Picasso fans. ⏱ *1 hr. 5 rue de Thorigny, 3rd.* ☎ *01-42-71-25-21. Admission 5€. Apr–Sept Wed–Mon 9:30am–7pm; Oct–Mar Wed–Mon 9:30am–5:30pm. Métro: St-Paul.*

**7** **Place des Vosges.** This is Paris's oldest square, and was once its most fashionable; today it's arguably its most adorable, with perfect brick-and-stone pavilions rising above covered arcades. Its

*The Picasso museum occupies the Hôtel Salé, built by a salt-tax collector.*

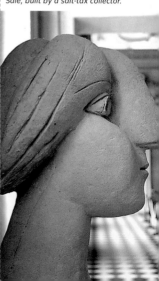

4<sup>me</sup>.ARR<sup>t</sup>

# PLACE DE LA BASTILLE

*This colorful street sign marks the birthplace of the French Revolution.*

perfect symmetry might be why so many writers and artists (Descartes, Pascal, Gautier, and Victor Hugo) chose to live here. *See p 14.*

**❽ Maison de Victor Hugo.** The writer of *I es Misérables* lived here from 1832 to 1848, and his home has been turned into a shrine of sorts. Love him or hate him, you have to admit Hugo was interesting. Cocteau called him a mad-man, and he may have had something there—in his old age, Hugo carved furniture with his teeth. In general, this is the usual tribute museum, with a few pieces he owned, including his inkwell and

some of his furniture (though the museum doesn't tell you how it was carved). ⏲ *15 min. 6 place des Vosges, 43.* ☎ *01-42-72-10-16. Free admission. Tues–Sun 10am–5:40pm. Métro: St-Paul or Bastille.*

**❾ ★ Place de la Bastille.** Nothing remains of the towered fortress that once stood here and held such prisoners as the "Man in the Iron Mask" and the Marquis de Sade. But it's worth a stop to commemorate the place where the Revolution began. *See p 14, bullet ❻.*

**❿ ★ Colonne de Juillet.** *See p 14, bullet ❼.*

*Victor Hugo.*

# Montmartre & the Sacré Coeur

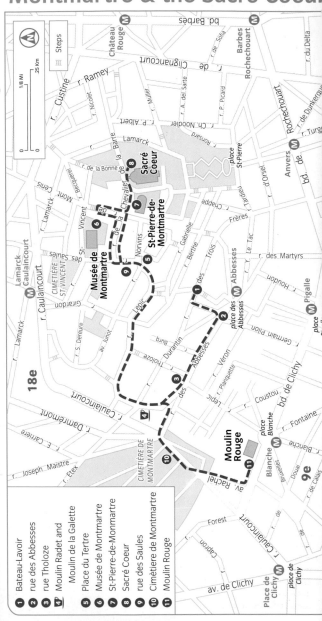

1 Bateau-Lavoir
2 rue des Abbesses
3 rue Tholoze
4 Moulin Radet and
   Moulin de la Galette
5 Place du Tertre
6 Musée de Montmartre
7 St-Pierre-de-Monmartre
8 Sacré Coeur
9 rue des Saules
10 Cimetière de Montmartre
11 Moulin Rouge

Artsy, graceful, undulating Montmartre does something to my heart. I can't explain it, but from the moment I see its narrow, tilting houses, still windmills and steep streets, I'm in love again. It all starts at the Abbesses Métro station—designed by French architect Hector Guimard, it's the only one in Paris with its original Beaux Arts glass roof. START: **Métro to Abbesses**

*Rue des Abbesses.*

**1 Bateau-Lavoir.** From the station, take rue Ravignan to place Emile-Godeau, where you'll find this building, called the "cradle of cubism." While living here (1904–12), Picasso painted *The Third Rose* (of Gertrude Stein) and *Les Demoiselles d'Avignon*. Today it's filled with art studios, some occasionally open to view. 🕐 *10 min. 13 place Emile Goudeau. Métro: Abbesses.*

**2 Rue des Abbesses.** Backtrack to the station, turn right, and head down this street. The unusual rust-red church on the left with the turquoise mosaics is the neo-Gothic St-Jean-de-Montmartre, built early in the 20th century. Peek inside to see its delicately weaving arches. Rue des Abbesses is lined with excellent cafes and wine bars.

**3 Rue Tholoze.** Rue des Abbesses soon brings you to this steep, narrow street, with an adorable windmill at the top. Halfway up is Studio 28, which was the city's first proper art-house cinema, named after the year in which it opened. It showed Buñuel's *L'Age d'Or* in 1930, and outraged locals ripped the screen from the wall. Today it still shows arty flicks and has a tiny bar.

**4 Moulin Radet & Moulin de la Galette.** When you reach the windmill, turn right down rue Lepic, which soon leads you to Moulin Radet, another of Montmartre's 30 windmills. The windmill sits above a restaurant called Le Moulin de la Galette which, confusingly, is named after a different, nearby windmill. The restaurant serves good, traditional French food at moderate prices. *83 rue Lepic.* ☎ *01-46-06-84-77. $$*

*Street performers congregate around Sacré Coeur and place du Tertre.*

*Ever-crowded place du Tertre.*

**5 Place du Tertre.** Climb the steep streets up to this old square, which might be lovely—I can never tell, what with all the tourists and the pesky artists chasing me around threatening to draw my caricature. You can buy some lovely original paintings here, but you'll have to barter to get a remotely reasonable price. The perpetual hubbub can be entertaining—it's charming and awful all at once.

*A Montmartre artist draws a customer's portrait.*

**6 Musée de Montmartre.** This isn't exactly a must-see, but if you're genuinely curious about the history of this neighborhood, it will give you a good look at its past. There are pictures of 19th-century Montmartre, rural and lined with windmills, along with a few Toulouse-Lautrec posters and the like. ⏱ *20 min. 12 rue Cortot, 8th.* ☎ *01-46-06-61-11. Admission 4.50€. Tues–Sun 10am–12:30pm, 1:30–6pm. Métro: Abbesses.*

**7 St-Pierre-de-Montmartre.** Follow the winding roads ever upwards to this old Benedictine abbey, now a small, early Gothic church. This is one of the city's most elderly churches (1133), as evidenced by its gradually bending columns. Its simplicity, in the shadow of an architectural giant, is refreshing. ⏱ *15 min. Rue du Mont-Cenis.*

**8 ★★ Sacré Coeur.** The creamy white domes of this basilica soar high above Paris. Inside is an artistic and archaeological explosion of color and form; out front are sweeping views of the gorgeous city in soft pastels. Unmissable. *See p 17.*

**9 Rue des Saules.** Head down rue des Saules, pausing to admire the oft-photographed nightclub Au Lapin Agile, which was a favorite hangout of Picasso's back when it was called Cabaret des Assassins. It's still usually crowded with tourists, strange fans of old French music, and those seeking Picasso's muse.

**10 ★★ Cimetière de Montmartre.** Follow rue Lepic back down past no. 54, where van Gogh lived with his brother Guillaumin. Turn right onto rue Joseph-de-Maistre, then left onto rue Caulaincourt to this quiet resting place. Get a map from the gatehouse (there's a stack on the desk)—it will help you find the graves of François Truffaut, Stendhal, Degas, and many others who rest here. But don't follow it too closely—it doesn't list most of the graceful statues of

*Emile Zola denounced Sacré Coeur as "the basilica of the ridiculous" for its fanciful architecture.*

*Dancer Vaslav Nijinsky's grave.*

exquisitely tragic women draped across tombs, nor does it tell you where the most beautiful trees stand, or where the light dapples through, just so. You'll have to discover those treasures on your own. ⏱ *1 hr. Access by stairs from rue Caulaincourt, 18th.* ☎ *01-43-87-64-24. Free admission. Mar 16–Nov 5 Mon–Fri 8am–6pm; Sat 8:30am–6pm; Sun 9am–6pm. Nov 6–Mar 15 Mon–Fri 8am–5:30pm; Sat 8:30am–5:30pm; Sun 9am–5:30pm. Métro: Blanche.*

**11 Moulin Rouge.** From the cemetery, take avenue Rachel, then turn left onto boulevard de Clichy to place Blanche, where you'll find the bright red windmill we all somehow know so well. Immortalized by Toulouse-Lautrec (and more recently, Nicole Kidman), it hasn't changed much with time. Just as the windmill remains outside, the cancan still goes on inside, and you can catch a lot of T & A, too. It's all just as tawdry and tacky as it was when Lautrec downed one absinthe after another to endure it. *See p 135.*

# Montparnasse

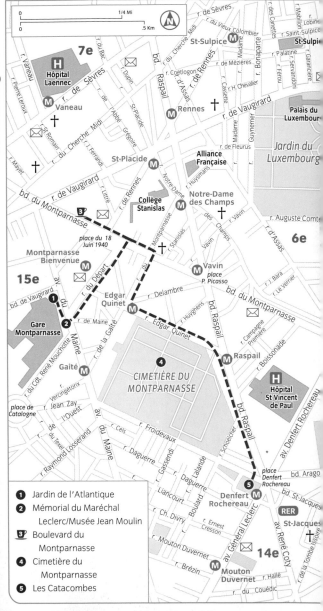

0       1/4 Mi
0            .5 Km

r. de Sèvres
r. du Vieux Colombier
**St-Sulpice** Ⓜ
**St-Sulpi**
r. des Canettes
r. Mabillon
r. Lobine
r. Saint-Sulpice
r. Palatine
r. Servandoni
r. Garancière
r. Ferou

r. du Bac
**7e**
Ⓗ
**Hôpital Laennec**
Ⓜ
**Vaneau**
r. du Cherche Midi
bd. Raspail
r. de Rennes
r. Coëtlogon
r. Madame
r. de Mézières
Bonaparte
r. H. Chevalier

r. Vaneau
r. Pierre Leroux
r. de Sèvres
r. de l'Abbé
r. St-Placide
r. Dupin
r. d'Assas
r. Cassette
r. de Vaugirard
Ⓜ **Rennes**
**Palais du Luxembour**

r. Mayet
r. Romain
r. du Cherche Midi
r. Ferrandi
Grégoire
Notre-Dame
r. Madame
Guynemer
r. de Fleurus
**Jardin du Luxembourg**

**St-Placide** Ⓜ
**Alliance Française**
r. Huysmans
r. de Vaugirard
**Collège Stanislas**
r. de Rennes
r. Littré
**Notre-Dame des Champs** Ⓜ
des Champs
r. Vavin
r. Auguste Comte

bd. du Montparnasse
③ ⊠
Montparnasse
r. Stanislas
Vavin
r. d'Assas
**6e**

place du 18 Juin 1940
**Montparnasse Bienvenue** Ⓜ
⊠
du Départ
du
Ⓜ **Vavin**
place P. Picasso
**15e**
av. du
r. du Départ
**Edgar Quinet**
r. Delambre
r. Huyghens
bd. du Montparnasse

① 
**Gare Montparnasse**
②
r. de Maine
Ⓜ **Edgar Quinet**
r. Campagne Première
⊠

r. du Cdt. René Mouchotte
Maine
r. de la Gaîté
r. Edgar Quinet
bd. Raspail
r. Boissonade
Ⓜ **Raspail**

**Gaîté** Ⓜ
r. Vercingétorix
④
**CIMETIÈRE DU MONTPARNASSE**
r. Huyghens
Ⓗ
**Hôpital St Vincent de Paul**

place de Catalogne
r. Jean Zay
av. de l'Ouest
r. Schœlcher
av. Denfert Rochereau

r. Raymond Losserand
av. du Maine
r. Cels
r. Froidevaux
r. Daguerre
r. Gassendi
bd. Raspail
place Denfert Rochereau
bd. Arago
bd. St-Jacques

r. de Texel
r. Daguerre
r. Lalande
r. Boulard
⑤
**Denfert Rochereau** Ⓜ
ℝ ℰ ℝ
**St-Jacques**

r. Liancourt
r. Ch. Divry
r. Ernest Cresson
av. du Général Leclerc
av. René Coty

r. Mouton Duvernet
r. Brézin
**Mouton Duvernet** Ⓜ
r. Hallé
**14e**
r. de la Tombe Issoire

① Jardin de l'Atlantique
② Mémorial du Maréchal Leclerc/Musée Jean Moulin
③ Boulevard du Montparnasse
④ Cimetière du Montparnasse
⑤ Les Catacombes
r. du Couëdic

When Montmartre artists did their jobs so well that the neighborhood became popular and rents finally went up, they all moved to Montparnasse. Before long Picasso, Léger, and Chagall had joined Man Ray, Henry Miller, and Gertrude Stein on its somewhat forbidding streets. In terms of beauty, the two areas don't compare—concrete is abundant in Montparnasse, but it offers plenty of sights to keep you busy. START: **Métro to Montparnasse-Bienvenue**

*Cafe life has thrived in Montparnasse since artists like Picasso moved here.*

**1 Jardin de l'Atlantique.** Built in 1995, this peaceful green retreat rises above the modern concrete, 6m (20 ft.) above the tracks where trains head out toward Brittany. ⏲ *30 min. Enter from Gare Montparnasse or place des Cinq-Martyrs-du-Lycée-Buffon, 15th. Daily dawn–dusk. Métro: Montparnasse-Bienvenue.*

**2 Mémorial du Maréchal Leclerc/Musée Jean Moulin.** In the same building as the Jardin de l'Atlantique, this rooftop museum will fill you in on World War II France and the French Resistance. The absorbing and educational film archives and the art—which includes posters exhorting residents of occupied France to work in Germany—show what the French endured. ⏲ *1 hr. Above Grandes*

*Lignes of Gare Montparnasse, 15th. ☎ 01-40-64-39-44. Free admission. Tues–Sun 10am–6pm. Métro: Montparnasse-Bienvenue.*

**3 Boulevard du Montparnasse.** Just a block from the train station, this well-traveled street gets busiest at night, when its cafes, brasseries, and cinemas are aglow, but at any time of day the enticing aromas may lure you to one of its many crêperies or cafes. Succumb to a full meal at no.108, Le Dôme, now a seafood restaurant, $$; or at no.102, La Coupole, a fabulous Art Deco brasserie, $$; or, a bit farther along, at no. 171, La Closerie des Lilas, which includes among its former fans an unlikely combination of Picasso, Trotsky, Lenin, and Hemingway, $$$.

*The Art Deco interior of La Coupole.*

Detail from a mausoleum in Montparnasse Cemetery.

**❹ ★ Cimetière du Montparnasse.** A short walk down boulevard Edgar Quinet, past its many attractive cafes, takes you to this well-known burial ground. Of the big three Parisian cemeteries (the other two being the Montmartre and the Père Lachaise), this is arguably at the bottom of the hierarchy, but for literary types and philosophical sorts, it's still a must-see. On its vast grounds are the graves of Samuel Beckett, Charles Baudelaire, and photographer Man Ray, as well as the shared grave of Simone de Beauvoir and Jean-Paul Sartre, usually covered in tiny notes of intellectual affection from fans. The delicate actress Jean Seberg, loved by Parisians for her role in *Breathless*, rests here too—peaceful at last. *3 bd. Edgar-Quenet, 14th.* ☎ *01-44-10-86-50. There's a map posted to the left of the main gate. Free admission. Mon–Fri 8am–6pm;*

*Sat 8:30am–6pm; Sun 9am–6pm. Métro: Edgar Quinet.*

**❺ ★★ kids Les Catacombes.** Just before the Revolution, in a sort of macabre urban renewal project, most of Paris's overcrowded cemeteries were emptied and all of the bones transferred underground into the crumbling Roman tunnels that sprawl beneath the city streets. It feels incredibly strange to visit rows of neatly stacked bones and skulls. There's a part of my brain that wants to convince me that this is art, when of course it isn't. The musty smell assures me of that, as does the sign near the appropriately dour entrance that reads STOP! THIS IS THE EMPIRE OF DEATH! Older kids will love it; younger ones will probably have nightmares. ◷ *1 hr. 1 place Denfert Rochereau, 14th.* ☎ *01-43-22-47-63. Admission 5€. Tues–Sun 10am–4pm. Métro: Denfert-Rochereau.* ●

*Some 50,000 visitors explore the ghoulish catacombs every year.*

# Shopping Best Bets

Best **Place to Find Chanel on Sale**
★★ Anna Lowe, *104 rue du Faubourg St-Honoré (p 86)*

Best **Flea Market**
Marché aux Puces de St-Ouen, *17 av. de la Porte de Clignancourt (p 82)*

Best **Contemporary Art**
★ Artcurial, *61 av. Montaigne (p 82)*

Best **Art Supplies**
★ Viaduc des Arts, *9–147 av. Daumesnil (p 82)*

Best **Children's Clothing**
★ Bonpoint, *15 rue Royale (p 83);* and Carabosse, *1 rue de Sevigne (p 83)*

Best **Toy Store**
Au Nain Bleu, *408 rue St-Honoré (p 83)*

Best **Place to Buy a Picnic Lunch**
★★★ Poilâne, *8 rue du Cherche-Midi (p 87)*

Best **Jewelry**
★★ Cartier, *23 place Vendôme (p 88)*

Best **Kitchenware**
E Dehillerin, *18 rue Coquilliére (p 88)*

Best **Place to Get Your Own Picasso**
Galerie 27, *27 rue de Seine (p 82)*

Best **Place for English-Language Books & Magazines**
Village Voice Bookshop, *6 rue Princesse (p 83)*

Best **Places to Shop for Gifts**
★ Baccarat, *11 place de la Madeleine (p. 85);* and Papeterie Moderne, *12 rue de la Ferronnerie (p 87)*

Best **Gourmet Food**
★ Fauchon, *26–30 place de la Madeleine (p 87)*

Best **Porcelain**
★★ Manufacture Nationale de Sèvres, *4 place André Malraux (p 86)*

Best **Place for a Princess**
Yves Saint Laurent, *19–21 av. Victor Hugo (p 86)*

Best **Place for a Makeover**
Makeup Forever Professional, *5 rue la Boétie (p 88)*

*Fauchon is the perfect place to sample rich fois gras.*

# Right Bank (8th & 16th–17th)

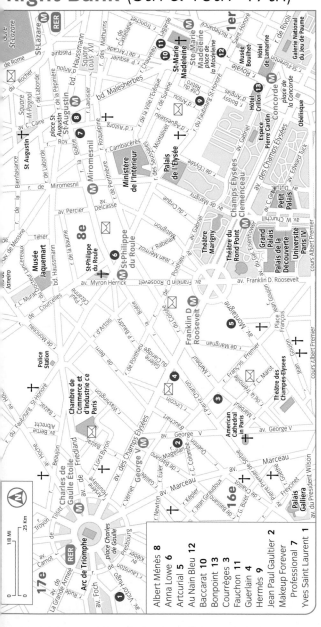

# Right Bank (1st–4th & 9th–11th)

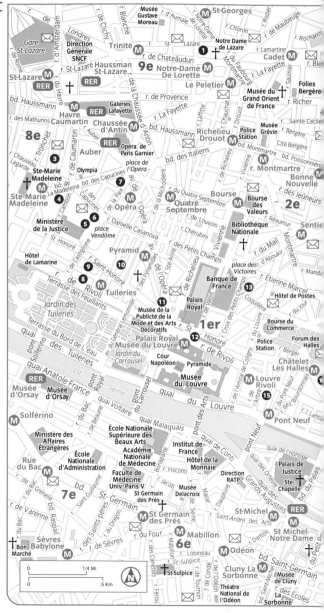

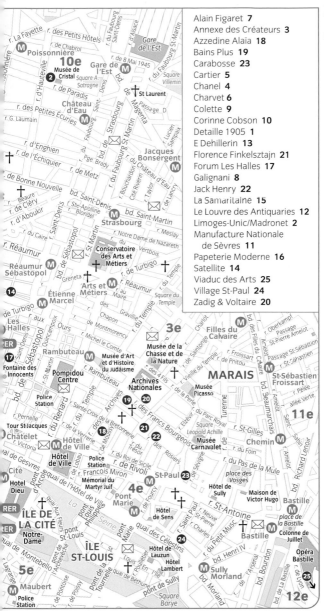

Alain Figaret **7**
Annexe des Créateurs **3**
Azzedine Alaïa **18**
Bains Plus **19**
Carabosse **23**
Cartier **5**
Chanel **4**
Charvet **6**
Colette **9**
Corinne Cobson **10**
Detaille 1905 **1**
E Dehillerin **13**
Florence Finkelsztajn **21**
Forum Les Halles **17**
Galignani **8**
Jack Henry **22**
La Samaritaine **15**
Le Louvre des Antiquaires **12**
Limoges-Unic/Madronet **2**
Manufacture Nationale
  de Sèvres **11**
Papeterie Moderne **16**
Satellite **14**
Viaduc des Arts **25**
Village St-Paul **24**
Zadig & Voltaire **20**

# Left Bank (5th–6th)

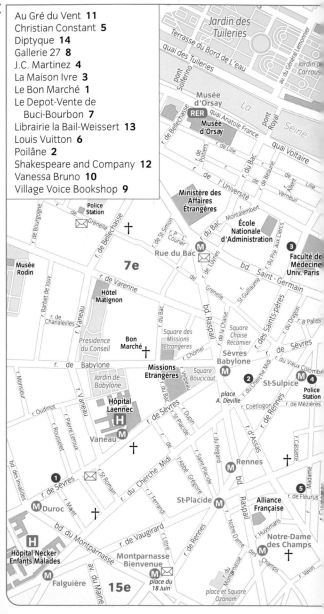

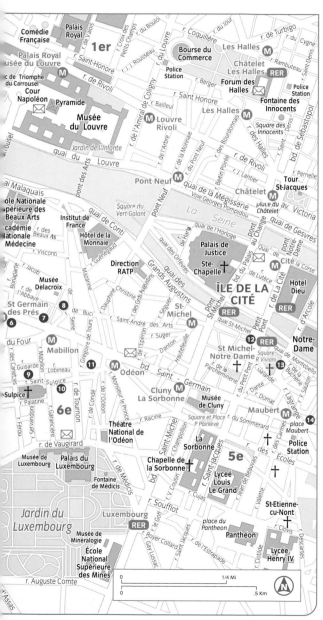

# Paris Shopping **A to Z**

## Antiques & Collectibles
### Le Louvre des Antiquaries
PALAIS ROYAL    Across from the Louvre, this palace of antiquity holds 250 vendors selling quality antiques from the 18th, 19th, and 20th centuries. Just the place if you seek 30 matching 19th-century Baccarat crystal champagne flutes, or a Sèvres tea set from 1773. Its selection of antique jewelry absolutely sparkles. *7 place du Palais Royal, 1st.* ☎ *01-42-07-07-27-00. MC, V. Métro: Palais Royal. Map p 78.*

### Marché aux Puces de St-Ouen
MONTMARTRE    This massive, permanent site, one of the largest flea markets in Europe, contains many 18th- and 19th-century treasures, but you'll have to hunt for them. *17 av. de la Porte de Clignancourt, 18th. No phone. No credit cards. Métro: Porte de Clignancourt.*

### Village St-Paul MARAIS    This
cluster of antiques dealers spreads across interlocking courtyards, selling quality early-20th-century furniture and art. *23–27 rue St-Paul, 4th. No phone. No credit cards. Métro: St-Paul. Map p 78.*

## Art
### ★ Artcurial CONCORDE    This is
the best, most prestigious place in Paris for contemporary art, from jewelry to sculpture to tapestry. *Centre d'Art Contemporain, 61 av. Montaigne, 8th.* ☎ *01-42-99-16-16. MC, V. Métro: Franklin-D.-Roosevelt. Map p 77.*

### Gallerie 27 ST-GERMAIN-DES-PRES
This tiny closet sells lithographs by early-20th-century artists including Picasso, Miró, and Léger, as well as works by contemporary artists. *27 rue de Seine, 6th.* ☎ *01-43-54-78-54.*

*MC, V. Métro: St-Germain-des-Prés or Odéon. Map p 80.*

### J. C. Martinez ST-GERMAIN-DES-
PRES    Tucked in a single room filled with more than 400 boxes, this quirky, fascinating gallery specializes in antique prints and engravings, some dating back to the 1700s. You can rummage through the inventory if you wish, or the excellent staff will point the way. *21 rue St-Sulpice, 6th.* ☎ *01-43-26-34-53. MC, V. Métro: Odéon or Mabillon. Map p 80.*

### ★ Viaduc des Arts BASTILLE
This complex of boutiques and crafts shops fills the vaulted space beneath a 19th-century railway access route into the Gare de Lyon with furniture makers, potters, glassblowers, and weavers. *9–147 av. Daumesnil, 12th.* ☎ *01-44-75-80-66. No credit cards. Métro: Bastille or Gare de Lyon. Map p 78.*

*A colorful jewelry display at Marché aux Puces de St-Ouen.*

## Books

**Galignani** TUILERIES This venerable wood-paneled bookstore, established in 1810, sells a vast selection of books in French and English. *224 rue de Rivoli, 1st.* ☎ *01-42-60-76-07. MC, V. Métro: Tuileries. Map p 78.*

**Librairie la Bail-Weissert** LATIN QUARTER Here you'll find one of Paris's best collections of atlases, rare maps, and engravings from the 15th to 19th centuries. *5 rue Lagrange, 5th.* ☎ *01-43-29-72-59. Métro: Maubert-Mutualité or St-Michel. Map p 80.*

**★★★ Shakespeare & Company** LATIN QUARTER The most famous bookstore in Paris was, in its early days, the literary home of Sylvia Beach, Hemingway, Fitzgerald, and Gertrude Stein. Expats still gather here to swap books and catch readings. *37 rue de la Bucherie, 5th.* ☎ *01-43-26-96–50. No credit cards. Métro: Maubert-Mutualité. Map p 80.*

**Village Voice Bookshop** LEFT BANK This quirky shop, another hangout of the expat literati, is an excellent source of English-language books and magazines. *6 rue Princesse, 6th.* ☎ *01-46-33-36-47. AE, DC, MC, V. Métro: Mabillon. Map p 80.*

## Children: Fashion & Toys

**Au Nain Bleu** CONCORDE You'll find everything their little hearts desire at the largest, oldest, and most central toy store in Paris—and possibly the poshest toy store in the world. *408 rue St-Honoré, 8th.* ☎ *01-42-60-39-01. AE, MC, V. Métro: Concorde or Madeleine. Map p 77.*

**★ Bonpoint** CONCORDE This place borders on haute couture for kids, so beware. The diminutive outfits are tailored, traditional, expensive, and irresistible. *15 rue Royale, 8th.* ☎ *01-47-42-52-63. AE, MC, V. Métro: Concorde. Map p 77.*

**Carabosse** MARAIS Fun, well-made outfits for babies and children who would like to look French. *1 rue de Sevigne, 4th.* ☎ *01-44-61-05-98. MC, V. Métro: St-Paul. Map p 78.*

## China, Crystal & Porcelain

**★ Baccarat** MADELEINE Baccarat, one of Europe's best-known purveyors of full-lead crystal, ensures that every pricey piece sparkles. But can your wallet take it? *11 place de la Madeleine, 8th.* ☎ *01-42-65-36-26. AE, MC, V. Métro: Madeleine. Map p 77.*

**La Maison Ivre** ST-GERMAIN-DE-PRES Handmade, country-style pottery fills this adorable shop. There's an emphasis on Provençal ceramics. *38 rue Jacob, 6th.* ☎ *01-42-60-01-85. MC, V. Métro: St-Germain-des-Prés. Map p 80.*

**Limoges-Unic/Madronet** BELLEVILLE This store is crammed with crystal by Daum, Baccarat, Lalique, Haviland, and Bernardaud,

*Baccarat has been around since 1764.*

along with glass and silver. *34 & 58 rue de Paradis, 10th.* ☎ *01-47-70-54-49. MC, V. Métro: Gare de l'Est. Map p 78.*

**★★ Manufacture Nationale de Sèvres** LES HALLES This is where the world-famous porcelain giant Sèvres sells the plates off which kings and presidents dine. *4 place André Malraux, 1st.* ☎ *01-47-03-40-20. MC, V. Métro: Palais Royal. Map p 78.*

### Department Stores

**Colette** LOUVRE This swank fashion citadel sells men's and women's fashions by some of the city's most promising young talent, including Marni and Lucien Pellat-Finet. For sophisticated shoppers with high credit card limits. For a reprieve, try the excellent tea shop. *213 rue St-Honoré, 1st.* ☎ *01-55-35-33-90. AE, MC, V. Métro: Tuileries or Pyramides. Map p 78.*

**Forum Les Halles** LES HALLES Once the site of a great produce market, Les Halles is now a vast metallic shopping mall crammed with chain stores. There's one of everything here, but the feel is very sterile, without a hint of *joie de vivre*. *1–7 rue Pierre-Lescot, 1st. No phone.*

*MC, V. Métro: Etienne-Marcel, Châtelet, or Les Halles. Map p 78.*

**La Samaritaine** LES HALLES Part of this venerable Art Nouveau/Art Deco–style mall is filled with affordable men's and women's fashions, and the rest with outrageously priced designer wares. *18 rue de la Monnaie, 1st.* ☎ *01-40-41-20-20. www.lasamaritaine.com. AE, DC, MC, V. Métro: Pont Neuf. Map p 78.*

**★ Le Bon Marché** INVALIDES Paris's oldest department store is jammed with luxury boutiques from Dior to Chanel, for both men and women. If you grow weary of the clothes, the Grande Epicerie food hall will dazzle you. *22–24 rue de Sevres, 7th.* ☎ *01-44-39-80-00. www.bonmarche.fr. AE, DC, MC, V. Métro: Sèvres-Babylone. Map p 80.*

### Fashion

**Alain Figaret** BOURSE One of France's foremost designers of men's shirts offers a broad range of fabrics and elegant silk ties. *21 rue de la Paix, 2nd.* ☎ *01-42-65-04-99. AE, MC, V. Métro: Opéra. Map p 78.*

**★★ Anna Lowe** MADELEINE Come here for designer clothing— Valentino, Thierry Mugler, Galliano,

*La Samaritaine's moderately priced, top-floor restaurant offers impressive city views.*

*Courrèges.*

Chanel—at discounts of up to 50%. *104 rue du Faubourg St-Honoré, 8th.* ☎ *01-42-66-11-32. MC, V. Métro: Miromesnil. Map p 77.*

### Annexe des Créateurs
MADELEINE   Few stores in Paris have received as much publicity in recent years as this high-end, discount women's-clothing outlet, where the collections of top-drawer designers are discounted as much as 70%. Expect Mugler, Versace, Moschino, Gaultier, and Vivienne Westwood. *19 rue Godot de Mauroy, 9th.* ☎ *01-42-65-46-40. www.annexedescreateurs.com. MC, V. Métro: Madeleine. Map p 78.*

### Au Gré du Vent
LATIN QUARTER   The diplomats and millionaires of Paris's female community come here (ever so discreetly) to sell their slightly worn couture on consignment. Heaven. *10 rue des Quatre Vents, 6th.* ☎ *01-44-07-28-73. MC, V. Métro: Odéon. Map p 80.*

### Azzedine Alaïa
MARAIS   Alaïa, known for bringing body consciousness back to French fashion (as if it had ever left), makes sexy clothes for skinny girls. If you can't swing the price tags, try the stock

shop around the corner at 18 rue de Verrerie. *7 rue de Moussy, 4th.* ☎ *01-42-72-19-19. MC, V. Métro: Hôtel-de-Ville. Map p 78.*

### ★★ Chanel
CONCORDE   This mother ship for lovers of Chanel's classic designs sits adjacent to the Chanel couture house (sigh) and behind the Ritz, where Coco Chanel lived. *Très chic, mes amis. 31 rue Cambon, 1st.* ☎ *01-42-86-26-00. AE, DC, MC, V. Métro: Concorde or Tuileries. Map p 78.*

### Charvet
OPERA   Charvet made shirts for fashionable Frenchmen for years before he was discovered by English royalty. (He now makes shirts for the duke of Windsor.) Shop here for crisp designs and lush fabrics for men and women. *28 place Vendôme, 1st.* ☎ *01-42-60-30-70. MC, V. Métro: Opéra. Map p 78.*

### Corinne Cobson
TUILERIES   A favorite of Paris's smart young set, Cobson uses simple lines and graphic prints to get her messages across. Anti-racism and pro-environment slogans decorate her low-necked T-shirts and chunky sweaters. *6 rue du Marché St-Honoré, 1st.* ☎ *01-42-60-48-64. AE, MC, V. Metro: Tuileries. Map p 78.*

### Courrèges
CONCORDE   Little white vinyl go-go boots, silver disco purses—here, it's the designer '70s again, with bold colors, plastic, and glitter. *40 rue François-1er, 8th.* ☎ *01-53-67-30-00. MC, V. Métro: Franklin-D.-Roosevelt. Map p 77.*

### Hermès
CONCORDE   France's single-most important status indicator is a Hermès scarf or tie. I'm sure the fact that they cost in excess of 240€ has nothing to do with it—it's probably all about the design. Come decide for yourself. *24 rue de Faubourg St-Honoré, 8th.*

*A gold-and-pearl Chanel pin.*

*Yves Saint Laurent broke into the fashion world in the 1970s with women's evening-wear designs.*

☎ 01-40-17-47-17. Métro: Concorde. AE, MC, V. Map p 77.

**Jack Henry** MARAIS New Yorker Henry has been perfecting his sparely cut suits in Paris for more than a decade now, and he's become one of the city's most sought-after designers of men's professional clothes. He favors a smooth, long line, and snug-fitting knits. *24 rue des Rosiers, 4th.* ☎ 01-44-59-89-44. AE, DC, MC, V. Métro: St-Paul. Map p 78.

**Jean-Paul Gaultier** MADELEINE It's all bustiers, straps, and fetish-chic as usual at this high-camp, high-fashion shop selling the wares of the "it" designer of the 1990s. *40 av. George V, 8th.* ☎ 01-44-43-00-44. AE, DC, MC, V. Métro: George-V. Map p 77.

**Le Depot-Vente de Buci-Bourbon** LATIN QUARTER This upscale boutique, one of the best consignment shops in the Latin Quarter, has plenty for both men and women, from Hermès scarves to Chanel shoes. *4–6 rue de Bourbon-de-Château, 6th.* ☎ 01-46-34-45-05. MC, V. Métro: Mabillon. Map p 80.

**Louis Vuitton** ST-GERMAIN-DES-PRES You already have the handbag, the wallet, the carry-on, or, you lucky devil, the suitcases with the famous insignia. But there's more! Monogrammed bags, posh pens, fine stationery . . . *6 place St-Germain-des-Prés, 6th.* ☎ 01-45-49-62-32. AE, MC, V. Métro: St-Germain-des-Prés. Map p 80.

**Vanessa Bruno** LATIN QUARTER Bruno's unique clothes are deeply feminine, without being frilly. Her years in Japan gave her an appreciation for sleek lines and simple, clean fabrics. Great bags, too. *4 rue St-Sulpice, 6th.* ☎ 01-43-54-41-04. AE, DC, MC, V. Métro: Odéon. Map p 80.

**Yves Saint Laurent** PASSY If you need a ball gown, ladies, this is where you go, no? Head to the branch at 12 place St-Sulpice, 6th (☎ 01-43-26-84-40) if you're interested in men's clothes as well. *19–21 av. Victor Hugo, 16th.* ☎ 01-45-00-64-64. AE, DC, MC, V. Métro: Etoile. Map p 77.

**Zadig & Voltaire** MARAIS This is one of six Z&V branches in Paris. Shelves are

*A signature Hermès scarf.*

stocked with hip clothes in classic styles for men and women. Cotton tops, cashmere sweaters, and faded jeans are big sellers. *41 rue des Francs-Bourgeois, 3rd.* ☎ *01-44-54-00-60. AE, MC, V. Métro: St-Paul or Hôtel-de-Ville. Map p 78.*

## Food

**Albert Ménès** MADELEINE One of Paris's most prestigious small-scale purveyors of foodstuffs prides itself on selling only goods that were picked, processed, and packaged by hand. Everything from sugared almonds to Breton sardines, terrines, jams, pâtés, and more. *41 bd. Malesherbes, 8th.* ☎ *01-42-66-95-63. MC, V. Métro: St-Augustin or Madeleine. Map p 77.*

**Christian Constant** LATIN QUARTER Chocoholics rejoice. The chocolates at this divine shop are made with exotic ingredients and sold by the kilo. *37 rue d'Assas, 6th.* ☎ *01-53-63-15-15. No credit cards. Métro: St-Placide. Map p 80.*

★ **Fauchon** MADELEINE This fabulous, upscale, mega-delicatessen will fill your stomach as fast as it empties your wallet. Must be seen to be believed. *26–30 place de la Madeleine, 8th.* ☎ *01-47-42-60-11. MC, V. Métro: Madeleine. Map p 77.*

★ **Florence Finkelsztajn** MARAIS This Jewish bakery, one of the best ethnic bakeries in the city, has all the heavy cakes, poppy seeds, apples, and cream cheese you could want. *27 rue des Rosiers, 4th.* ☎ *01-42-72-78-91. No credit cards. Métro: St-Paul. Map p 78.*

★★★ **Poilâne** ST-GERMAINE-DES-PRES One of the city's best-loved bakeries, with irresistible apple tarts, butter cookies, and crusty croissants. Get in line. *8 rue du Cherche-Midi, 6th.* ☎ *01-45-48-42-59. No credit cards. Métro: St-Sulpice. Map p 80.*

## Gifts

**Diptyque** ST-GERMAIN-DES-PRES You may have seen these pricey, scent-infused candles in upscale stores in the U.S. and the U.K. Come here to sample the 53 scents. *46 bd. St-Germain, 5th.* ☎ *01-43-26-45-27. AE, MC, V. Métro: Maubert-Mutualité. Map p 80.*

**Papeterie Moderne** CHATELET This is a great shop for little gifts, like enamel plaques based on those you see on Parisian streets and court-yard gateways. So cute. *12 rue de la Ferronnerie, 1st.* ☎ *01-42-36-21-72. No credit cards. Métro: Châtelet. Map p 78.*

*The Florence Finkelsztajn store window.*

*Cartier makes a great window-shopping stop even if you're not in the market for jewels.*

## Jewelry

★★ **Cartier** CONCORDE One of the most famous jewelers in the world, Cartier has glamorous gems to match its sky-high prices. *23 place Vendôme, 1st.* ☎ *01-44-55-32-50. AE, MC, V. Métro: Opéra or Tuileries. Map p 78.*

★ **Satellite** GRANDS BOULEVARDS Stylist Sandrine Dulon uses high-quality stones from Bavaria in intricate earrings, bracelets, and necklaces priced from 10€ to 700€. *10 rue Dussoubs, 2nd (near rue Marie Stuart).* ☎ *01-55-34-95-70. AE, MC, V. Métro: Réaumur-Sébastopol. Map p 78.*

## Kitchen & Bathroom

**Bains Plus** MARAIS Men come here to treat themselves to posh shaving soap, razors, manly loofah sponges, darling-I-mean-handsome bathrobes, and unguents galore. *51 rue des Francs-Bourgeois, 4th.* ☎ *01-48-87-83-07. AE, MC, V. Métro: Hôtel-de-Ville. Map p 78.*

**E Dehillerin** LES HALLES This shop has outfitted great chefs for more than a century. Nothing here comes cheap, but a Dehillerin sauté pan is forever. *18 rue Coquillière, 1st.* ☎ *01-42-36-53-13. MC, V. Métro: Les Halles. Map p 78.*

## Perfume & Makeup

**Detaille 1905** PIGALLE Step back in time in this perfumery, where six key fragrances have been flying off the shelves for a century. *10 rue St-Lazare, 9th.* ☎ *01-48-78-68-50. www.detaille.com. MC, V. Métro: Notre-Dame-de-Lorette. Map p 78.*

**Guerlain** MADELEINE This adorable Belle Epoque boutique sells skin cream, perfume, cosmetics, and more. Divine. *68 av. des Champs-Elysées, 8th.* ☎ *01-45-62-52-57. www.guerlain.fr. AE, MC, V. Métro: Franklin-D.-Roosevelt. Map p 77.*

**Makeup Forever Professional** MADELEINE This is where models go to buy their own makeup, so why shouldn't you? Staff members are helpful, the makeup is fierce, and you'll look like a glamour-puss. *5 rue La Boétie, 8th.* ☎ *01-42-66-01-60. AE, DC, MC, V. Métro: Miromesnil. Map p 77.* ●

# 5 The Best of the **Outdoors**

# Jardin des Tuileries

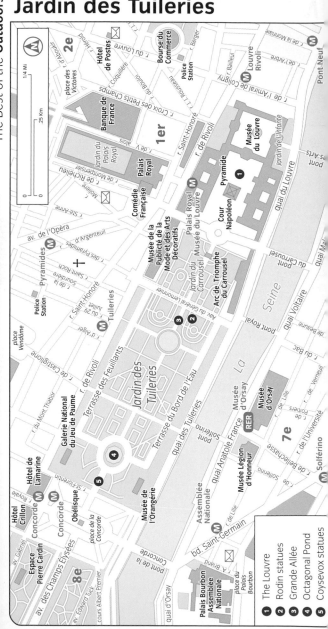

1 The Louvre
2 Rodin statues
3 Grande Allée
4 Octagonal Pond
5 Coysevox statues

**M**ore a statue garden than, as it names implies, a "garden of tiles" (the clay earth here was once used to make roof tiles), the Tuileries stretch from the Louvre all the way down to the place de la Concorde. Under lacy chestnut trees, paths curl and stretch off the dusty main *allée* (alley), and each seems to hold something to charm you—statues, ice-cream stands, ponds, and shaded tables where you can spread out and rest. It's open daily, from 7am to 9pm in summer, and from 7am to 8pm in winter. START: **Métro to Tuileries or Concorde**

**❶ The Louvre.** Start in the court-yard. The gold-tipped obelisk you can see gleaming at the end of the gardens (the Luxor Obelisk, a gift from Egypt) marks place de la Concorde. As you walk into the garden you'll pass buskers selling cheap, imported Eiffel Towers, and you'll be pestered by artists who insist you're so beautiful they simply must paint you. Everybody will talk to you in English ("Hey lady! Lady! Look here!") without asking first what language you speak—you get the picture.

**❷ Rodin Statues.** Extricate yourself from the crowds and keep walking until you cross avenue du Général-Lemonnier. Four typically graceful statues by Rodin (*The Kiss*, *Eve*, *Meditation*, and *The Shadow*) flank the wide central path. The glimmering, golden statue in the distance at place des Pyramides is *Joan of Arc*.

**❸ Grande Allée.** Off to the sides of the Grande Allée, a number of modern statues peek at you from the greenery—Henry Moore's *Figure Couchée* lounges leisurely, and Alberto Giacometti's *Grande Femme II* sits near Jean Dubuffet's dazzling *Le Bel Costume*. One of my favorites is *The Welcoming Hands*—a collage of intertwined hands, by Louise Bourgeois.

**❹ Octagonal Pond.** The statues surrounding this pond date to the days when this was a royal park fronting the ill-fated Palais Tuileries, which burned to the ground during a battle in 1871. The statues are all allegories—of the seasons, of French rivers, of the Nile, and of the Tiber.

**❺ Coysevox Statues.** At the end of the garden, at the gates facing the place de la Concorde, are copies of a set of elaborate statues originally created by Louis XIV's sculptor, Charles-Antoine Coysevox (1640–1720). They depict the gods Mercury and Fame riding winged horses.

*Le Nôtre, who designed the Versailles grounds, also designed the Tuileries.*

# Cimetière du Père-Lachaise

1. Main Entrance
2. Colette
3. Gioacchio Antonio Rossini
4. Hèloïse and Abelard
5. Jim Morrison
6. Frédéric Chopin
7. Georges Bizet
8. Honoré de Balzac
9. Eugène Delacroix
10. Marcel Proust
11. Isadora Duncan
12. Oscar Wilde
13. Gertrude Stein
14. Edith Piaf
15. Exit

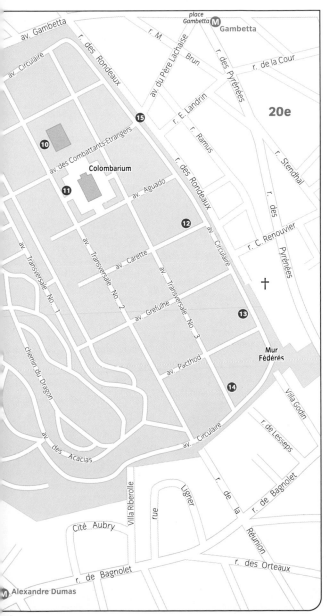

**P**ère-Lachaise became one of the world's most famous cemeteries when Jim Morrison died (or didn't die, as some fans believed) in 1971. Almost immediately Morrison's grave became a site of pilgrimage, and the place filled with tourists, most of whom you can avoid if you stay away from Morrison's grave. START: Métro to Philippe-Auguste or Père-Lachaise

**1 Main Entrance.** Start by picking up a free map at the gate. *Bd. de Ménilmontant & rue de la Roquette.* ☎ *01-55-25-8-2-10. Free admission. Daily 8:30am–6pm. Métro: Philippe-Auguste or Père-Lachaise.*

**2 Colette.** French writer Sidonie-Gabrielle Colette published 50 novels. Her most famous story, *Gigi*, became a successful Broadway play and film. When she died in 1954, she was given a state funeral but was refused Roman Catholic rites because of her naughty lifestyle. *Section 4.*

**3 Gioacchio Antonio Rossini.** The Italian musical composer is best known for *The Barber of Seville* and *William Tell*, the overture of which is one of the most famous in the world. His dramatic style led to his nickname among other composers— "Monsieur Crescendo." *Section 4.*

**4 Hèloïse & Abelard.** If you turn right down avenue du Puits, near Colette's grave, you soon come to the oldest inhabitants of the cemetery. These star-crossed medieval lovers were kept apart their entire lives by Hèloïse's family. Their passionate love letters to one another were published and have survived the ages. Abelard died first. Local lore maintains that when Hèloïse died, a romantic abbess opened Abelard's grave to put Hèloïse's body inside, and his corpse opened its arms to embrace his long-lost love. *Section 7.*

**5 Jim Morrison.** If you must visit Morrison's grave, follow the crowds. The bust that once stood at the head of the tomb was stolen years ago by one of his "fans." The cigarette butts stubbed out in the grave are also courtesy of his "fans." As

*The city acquired the cemetery in 1804; 19th-century sculpture abounds.*

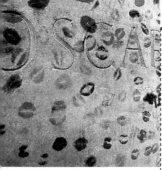

*Lipstick kisses cover Oscar Wilde's tombstone.*

are the graffiti and the stench of old beer. What a mess. *Section 6.*

**⑥ Frédéric Chopin.** Retrace your steps across avenue Casimir-Perier to section 11, where you'll find the appropriately elaborate grave of Chopin marked with a statue of Erato, the muse of music. *Section 11.*

**⑦ Georges Bizet.** The bespectacled 19th-century composer of *Carmen* was a child prodigy who entered the prestigious Paris Conservatory of Music at age 9. *Section 68.*

**⑧ Honoré de Balzac.** The passionate French novelist wrote for up to 15 hours a day, drinking prodigious quantities of coffee to keep him going. His writing was often sloppy and uninspired, but it makes an excellent record of 19th-century Parisian life. *Section 48.*

**⑨ Eugène Delacroix.** This dramatic and intensely romantic painter's *Liberty Leading the People* is a lesson in topless inspiration. His bizarre phallic tomb puzzles and vaguely horrifies me each time I see it. *Section 49.*

**⑩ Marcel Proust.** The wistful 19th-century novelist died before he could finish editing his famous series of books, *A la Recherche du Temps Perdu (Remembrance of Things*

*Past),* yet he's considered one of the world's great writers. *Section 85.*

**⑪ Isadora Duncan.** The tragic death of this marvelous modern dancer is legendary—she favored long, dramatic scarves and convertibles, and one day one of those wrapped around the other and that was the end of Isadora. *Section 87.*

**⑫ Oscar Wilde.** The bluntly named avenue des Etrangers Morts pour la France (Avenue of Dead Foreigners, basically) leads you to the fantastical tomb of this gay 19th-century wit and writer. The size of the member with which the artist equipped the statue was quite the buzz in Paris until a vengeful woman knocked it off. *Section 89.*

**⑬ Gertrude Stein.** The early-20th-century writer and unlikely artistic muse shares a simple, double-sided tomb with her longtime companion, Alice B. Toklas. *Section 94.*

**⑭ Edith Piaf.** Just one more stop before you collapse—the resting place of famed French songbird Edith Piaf, beloved by brokenhearted lovers and gay men everywhere. *Section 97.*

**⑮ Exit.** Leave the cemetery at rue de la Réunion, and from there head to the Alexandre Dumas Métro station (or the nearest wine bar).

*Fans often leave mementos on Edith Piaf's grave.*

# Exploring **Bois de Boulogne**

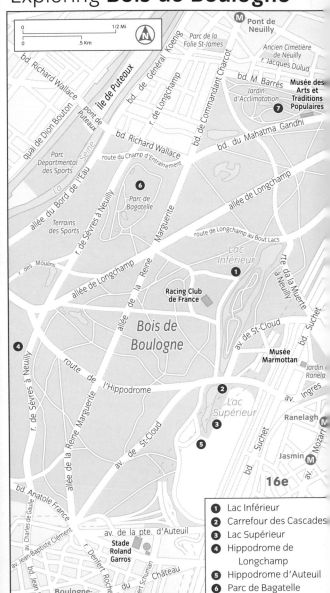

1. Lac Inférieur
2. Carrefour des Cascades
3. Lac Supérieur
4. Hippodrome de Longchamp
5. Hippodrome d'Auteuil
6. Parc de Bagatelle
7. Jardin d'Acclimation

**T**his former forest, once used for royal hunts, has two personalities. By day it's a family park where children gambol and adults rattle along in horse-drawn carriages, taking in the beauty of its lakes and waterfalls. By night it's one of the city's busiest prostitution districts and a hub for other nefarious activities not recommended for those who do not want to know what the inside of a French jail looks like. In other words, do visit, but get out before sunset. The park is so big that you'll probably have to catch a cab or hitch a ride on one of the horse-drawn carriages to get from one end of the park to the other. Otherwise you'll be limited by the sheer size of the place. START: **RER to avenue Foch**

**1 Lac Inférieur.** I prefer to enter the park by way of avenue Foch because it I keep going straight, I'm soon at this unfairly named lake. Its two islands are connected by fanciful footbridges. You can rent boats and paddle across to the islands' cafes and restaurants. On a hot summer day, I can't think of a better place to be in Paris.

**2 Carrefour des Cascades.** The scenic walkway between the upper and lower lakes is an attraction in itself, with willows dipping their branches languorously in the water, and a handsome, man-made waterfall creating a gorgeous backdrop. You can even walk under the waterfall if you want.

**3 Lac Supérieur.** The larger of the two lakes has more of everything you find on the smaller lake, with lots of boats to paddle and several restaurants and cafes dotted about.

**4 Hippodrome de Longchamp.** If your euros are burning a hole in your pocket, head to the southern end of the park, where two horse-racing courses— the excellent Hippodrome de Longchamp and the smaller Hippodrome d'Auteuil (see next stop)— offer galloping action. The Grand Prix held at Longchamp each June is the equivalent of the Kentucky Derby, and gets the ladies out to the track in their finest hats. Check the website for dates of

*Paddling around Bois de Boulogne's lakes is a perfect pastime for a hot day.*

*Rose bushes in Parc de Bagatelle.*

other races. ☎ 01-44-20-75-00.
www.france-galop.com. Métro: Porte
Maillot.

**⑤ Hippodrome d'Auteuil.**
This racetrack, the smaller of the
two in Bois de Boulogne, is known
for its steeplechases and obstacle
courses. It's a long walk from the
other Hippodrome, so I recommend
catching a cab or carriage. ☎ 01-
40-71-47-47. www.france-galop.com.
Métro: Porte Auteuil.

**⑥ Parc de Bagatelle.** Take a
cab or carriage to this park-within-
a-park. The northwestern section of
Bois de Boulogne is a riot of colorful
tulips in spring, and the rose garden
blooms spectacularly by late May.
This is one of Paris's most popular
trysting spots, and it's fairly easy to
see why. ☎ 01-40-67-97-00.

**⑦ ★★ kids Jardin d'Acclimata-
tion.** Those with small children may
want to skip the rest of this tour and
head straight here. (If you come
from Parc de Bagatelle, you should
probably take a cab or carriage.)
This amusement park on the north
end of Bois de Boulogne boasts
colorful rides, a small zoo, and a
kid-size train. See p 43, bullet ⑥. ●

# Bois de Boulogne: Practical Matters

Bois de Boulogne is open daily from dawn to dusk. Because it's
such a large park, there are several entrances and several public
transportation options. Nearby Métro stops include Les Sablons
(north, on av. Charles de Gaulle), Porte Maillot (northeast, on av. de
la Grande Armée), Porte Dauphine (northeast, on av. Foch), or Porte
d'Auteuil (southeast, on av. de la Porte d'Auteuil). Take the RER to
avenue Foch or avenue Henri Martin. In the park are numerous cafes
and restaurants. A miniature train runs to the Jardin d'Acclimation
from Porte Maillot. Horse-drawn carriages operate around the park
as well—you'll see them lined up, waiting for riders. Carriage rides
cost 15€ to 25€.

# **Dining** Best Bets

Best **for Cheese-a-holics**
★ Androuët sur le Pouce $$ *49 rue St-Roch (p 106)*

Best **for High Society**
★ Angélina $$ *226 rue de Rivoli (p 106)*

Best **for Kids**
★ Breakfast in America $ *17 rue des Ecoles (p 107)*

Best **Good Cheap Meal in Expensive Surroundings**
★ Chartier $$ *7 rue du Faubourg Montmartre (p 108)*

Best **Comfort Food**
★★ Chez Georges $$$ *1 rue du Mail (p 108)*

Best **Vegetarian**
★★ Piccolo Teatro $$ *6 rue des Ecouffes (p 110)*

Best **Seafood**
★ Iode $$$ *48 rue d'Argout (p 109)*

Best **for Sheer Beauty**
★★★ Les Elysées du Vernet $$$$$ *In the Hôtel Vernet, 25 rue Vernet (p 110)*

Best **Healthy Lunch**
Foody's Brunch Café $ *26 rue Montorgueil (p 108)*

Best **for Food Critics**
★★★ Le Grand Véfour $$$$$ *17 rue de Beaujolais (p 110)*

Best **Home-Style Cooking**
★ The Kitchen $$ *153 rue Montmartre (p 109)*

Best **for Something Offal**
Mimosa $$ *44 rue d'Argout (p 111)*

Best **Late-Night Snack**
Le Petit Marché $$$ *9 rue de Béarn (p 110)*

Best **Star Spotting**
La Poule au Pot $$$ *9 rue Vauvilliers (p 109)*

Best **Celebrity-Chef Restaurant**
★★★ Restaurant Plaza Athénée (Alain Ducasse) $$$$$ *In the Plaza Athénée hotel, 25 av. Montaigne (p 112)*

Best **Dining with a View**
★★ La Tour d'Argent $$$$$ *15–17 quai de la Tournelle (p 110)*

Best **When Money is No Object**
★★★ Taillevent $$$$$ *15 rue Lamennais (p 112)*

*You can sample sweet or savory crepes at cafes, bistros, and stands all over Paris.*

# Right Bank (8th & 16th–17th)

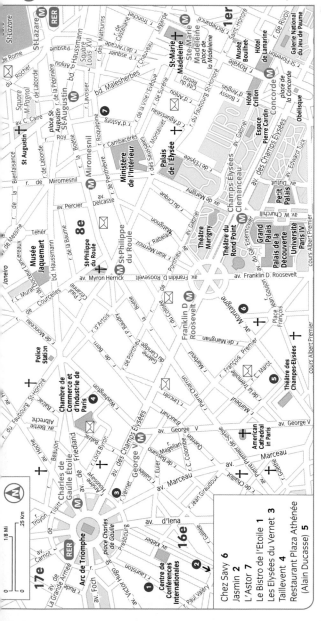

Chez Savy **6**
Jasmin **2**
L'Astor **7**
Le Bistro de l'Etoile **1**
Les Elysées du Vernet **3**
Taillevent **4**
Restaurant Plaza Athénée (Alain Ducasse) **5**

# Right Bank (1st–4th & 9th–11th

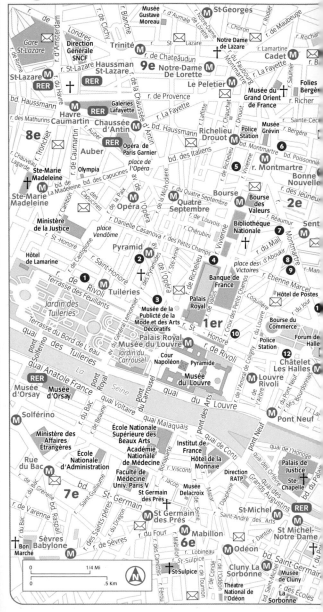

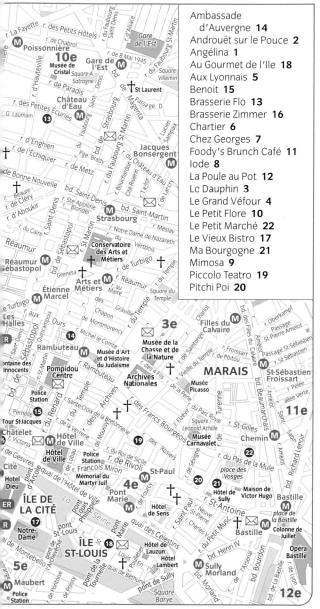

Ambassade
  d'Auvergne **14**
Androuët sur le Pouce **2**
Angélina **1**
Au Gourmet de l'Ile **18**
Aux Lyonnais **5**
Benoit **15**
Brasserie Flo **13**
Brasserie Zimmer **16**
Chartier **6**
Chez Georges **7**
Foody's Brunch Café **11**
Iode **8**
La Poule au Pot **12**
Lc Dauphin **3**
Le Grand Véfour **4**
Le Petit Flore **10**
Le Petit Marché **22**
Le Vieux Bistro **17**
Ma Bourgogne **21**
Mimosa **9**
Piccolo Teatro **19**
Pitchi Poi **20**

# Left Bank (5th–6th)

Musée
du Louvre

1er

Musée
d'Orsay

quai Voltaire

quai du Louvre

La Seine

quai Malaquais

pont du Carrousel

pont des Arts

quai du Louvre

r. du Bac

de Beaune

de Lille

Allent

Verneuil

École Nationale
Supérieure des
Beaux Arts

Institut de
France

Square du
Vert-Galant

quai de Conti

Montalembert

Académie
Nationale
de Médecine

Square
H Champion

r. des
Beaux Arts

Hôtel de la
Monnaie

École
Nationale
d'Administration

r. du Pré
aux Clercs

Faculté de
Médecine
Univ. Paris V

Bonaparte

r. Visconti

r. Jacob

r. Guénégaud

Direction
RATP

7e

Saint-Guillaume

bd. St-Germain

Saint Benoît

Musée
Delacroix

r. de l'Abbaye

de l'Échaudé

Seine

de

Mazarine

R. Dauphine

Christine

R. des Gds Augustins

de Grenelle

r. des Saints-Pères

r. du Dragon

St Germain
Des Prés M

St Germain
des Prés M

r. B Palissy

r. de Buci

r. Grégoire de Tours

de l'Éperon

Square Chaise
Récamier

r. du Four

Bonaparte

r. des Canettes

r. Mabillon

Mabillon M

bd. Saint-Germain

Sèvres
Babylone M

r. de Sèvres

r. du Vieux Colombier

r. Guisarde

r. Lobineau

Odéon M

r. du Cherche Midi

St-Sulpice

Police
Station

r. Saint-Sulpice

r. de Tournon

r. de l'Odéon

Monsieur le Prince

place
A. Deville ❷

r. Coëtlogon

r. de Mézières

† St-Sulpice

r. P. Palatine

r. Garancière

r. Férou

r. Servandoni

r. de Condé

Théâtre
National de
l'Odéon

6e

r. de Rennes

allée du Séminaire

r. H. Chevalier

Madame

r. d'Assas

M Rennes

r. Cassette

r. de Vaugirard

Musée de
Luxembourg

Palais du
Luxembourg

Fontaine
de Médicis

de Médicis

†

r. de Fleurus

r. Guynemer

Jardin du
Luxembourg

Luxembourg
RER

Alliance
Française

r. Huysmans

r. Madame

r. d'Assas

Musée de
Minéralogie

bd. Raspail

Notre-Dame
des Champs

Notre-Dame des Champs

M

place et Square
Ozanam

r. du Montparnasse

bd. Raspail

r. Stanislas

r. Vavin

École
National
Supérieure
des Mines

r. Auguste Comte

bd. St-Michel

Luxembourg
RER

❶

0                    1/4 Mi

0          .25 Km

N

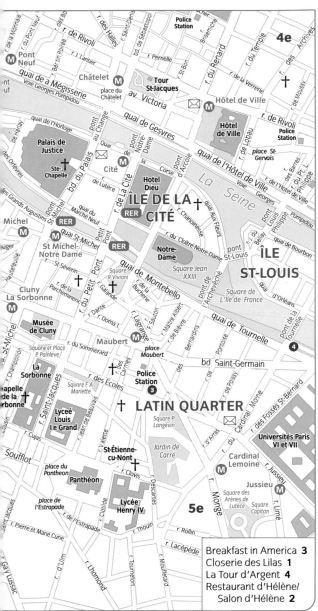

Breakfast in America **3**
Closerie des Lilas **1**
La Tour d'Argent **4**
Restaurant d'Hélène/
Salon d'Hélène **2**

# Paris Restaurants **A to Z**

You're likely to catch fashion-industry mavens having a cuppa at Angélina.

### ★★ Ambassade d'Auvergne

BEAUBOURG *TRADITIONAL FRENCH*
Traditional French goes a bit elegant at this friendly restaurant. Try the house special of lentils cooked in goose fat (it tastes better than it sounds), beef stewed in red wine, and rich and gooey *aligot* (potatoes and cheese). *22 rue du Grenier St-Lazare, 3rd.* ☎ *01-42-72-31-22. www.ambassade-auvergne.com. Entrees 25€–34€. MC, V. Lunch & dinner daily; closed Sun July 14–Aug 15. Métro: Rambuteau. Map p 102.*

### ★ kids Androuët sur le Pouce

TUILERIES *CHEESE* This unique and reliably good restaurant specializes in meals with cheese as the main ingredient. Good bets include the ravioli, the *tartines* (open-face sandwiches), and the huge cheese platters. *49 rue St-Roch, 1st.* ☎ *01-42-97-57-39. Entrees*

*12€–23€. MC, V. Lunch & dinner daily. Métro: Pyramides. Map p 102.*

### ★ Angélina TUILERIES *TEA SHOP*

This traditional *salon de thé* serves its high-society patrons tea, pastries, and sandwiches on silver platters. Dress up. *226 rue de Rivoli, 1st.* ☎ *01-42-60-82-00. Tea 6€–11€; entrees 12€–15€. AE, MC, V. Breakfast, lunch & tea daily (until 7pm). Métro: Tuileries or Concorde. Map p 102.*

### ★★ Au Gourmet de l'Ile ILE

ST-LOUIS *TRADITIONAL FRENCH*
Meals here are traditional pleasures, served in a beautiful setting, with beamed ceilings and candlelit tables. Try the chitterling sausages, savory pork with onions, or stuffed mussels in shallot butter. *42 rue St-Louis-en-l'Ile, 4th.* ☎ *01-43-26-79-27. Reservations required. Entrees 17€–22€; prix-fixe menu 33€. Lunch & dinner Wed–Sun. Métro: Pont Marie. Map p 102.*

### ★ Aux Lyonnais GRANDS BOULE-

VARDS *LYONNAIS* Famed chef

The morning market's freshest finds are served up at Aux Lyonnais.

*Brasserie Flo has changed little since it opened in 1860.*

Alain Ducasse, the best in Paris at Lyonnais cuisine, creates dishes like parsleyed calf's liver, pike dumplings, skate meunière, and peppery *coq au vin* in a restaurant designed to look like a 19th-century bistro. *32 rue St-Marc, 2nd.* ☎ *01-42-96-65-04. Reservations required. Prix-fixe menu 18€–32€. AE, DC, MC, V. Lunch & dinner Tues–Fri; dinner Sat. Métro: Grands Boulevards. Map p 102.*

★ **Benoit** MARAIS *TRADITIONAL FRENCH* Since 1912 every mayor of Paris has dined at Benoit; perhaps that explains the air of gravitas here. Time-tested classics fill the menu— my favorites are the escargot, cassoulet, and for dessert, Sainte-Eve (pears with cream). *20 rue St-Martin, 4th.* ☎ *01-42-72-25-76. Reservations required. Entrees 50€–120€; prix-fixe lunch 38€. Lunch & dinner daily. Métro: Hôtel-de-Ville. Map p 102.*

★★ **Brasserie Flo** NORTHEAST PARIS *TRADITIONAL FRENCH* This well-known restaurant is a bit hard to find, but you'll be glad you tracked it down when you try the onion soup, sole meunière, or guinea hen with lentils. *Formidable. 7 cour des Petites-Ecuries, 10th.* ☎ *01-47-70-13-59. Reservations recommended. Entrees 16€–24€; prix fixe 23€ lunch, 33€ dinner.*

*AE, DC, MC, V. Lunch & dinner daily. Métro: Château d'Eau or Strasbourg-St-Denis. Map p 102.*

**Brasserie Zimmer** CONCORDE *TRADITIONAL FRENCH* Stop by this centrally located, trendy brasserie to linger over the green salad with duck breast, then move on to main courses like the chateaubriand with béarnaise sauce, or the seafood mixed grill. *1 place du Châtelet, 1st.* ☎ *01-42-36-74-03. www.lezimmer. com. Entrees 12€–18€; prix fixe 20€. AE, MC, V. Dinner daily. Métro: Châtelet. Map p 102.*

★ **kids** **Breakfast in America** LATIN QUARTER *AMERICAN* Homesick Americans make a beeline to this diner, which could have been transported here straight from the streets of Chicago. The menu features favorites like pancakes with maple syrup, fresh-squeezed OJ, burgers with grilled onions and fries, and brownies. *17 rue des Ecoles, 5th.* ☎ *01-43-54-50-28. www. breakfast-in-america.com. Entrees 7€–12€. MC, V. Breakfast, lunch & dinner daily. Métro: Cardinal Lemoine. Map p 104.*

*Crowds pack in for hearty meals at Breakfast in America.*

★ **Chartier** LES HALLES *TRADITIONAL FRENCH*   This unpretentious, affordable, *fin-de-siècle* restaurant has soaring ceilings, fabulous brasswork, and straightforward cooking—try the beef *bourguignon* (in red-wine sauce), the *pavé* (thick steak), or the fish. *7 rue du Faubourg Montmartre, 9th.* ☎ *01-47-70-86-29. Entrees 9.50€–18€. MC, V. Lunch & dinner daily. Métro: Grands Boulevards. Map p 102.*

★★ **Chez Georges** BOURSE *TRADITIONAL FRENCH*   This is what the French call *la cuisine bourgeoise* (comfort food). Try the sweetbreads with morels, duck breast with *cèpes* (porcini mushrooms), cassoulet, or sole with wine sauce. *1 rue du Mail, 2nd.* ☎ *01-42-60-07-11. Reservations required. Entrees 25€–27€. AE, MC, V. Lunch & dinner Mon–Sat. Closed 3 weeks in Aug. Métro: Bourse. Map p 102.*

★ **Chez Savy** MADELEINE *RURAL FRENCH*   This 1920s bistro boasts original architectural details and offers hearty food like slow-cooked lamb with rosemary, served with *petit farçou* (thick crepes with vegetables). *23 rue Bayard, 8th.* ☎ *01-47-23-46-98. Reservations recommended. Entrees 23€–28€;*

*prix fixe 20€–24€ lunch, 27€ dinner. AE, MC, V. Lunch & dinner Mon–Fri. Closed Aug. Métro: Franklin-D.-Roosevelt. Map p 101.*

★ **Closerie des Lilas** LATIN QUARTER *TRADITIONAL FRENCH*   This restaurant and brasserie was a favorite of Gertrude Stein and Picasso (not to mention Lenin and Trotsky—a revolution marches on its stomach, apparently). Have a champagne julep before stuffing yourself with veal ribs with cider, or filet of beef in peppercorn sauce. *171 bd. du Montparnasse, 6th.* ☎ *01-40-51-34-50. Reservations far in advance for the restaurant, not needed for the brasserie. Entrees at the restaurant 35€–45€, at the brasserie 19€–24€. AE, DC, V. Lunch & dinner daily. Métro: Port Royal or Vavin. Map p 104.*

**kids** **Foody's Brunch Café** LES HALLES *VEGETARIAN*   They mean lunch, really. This is a good, reliable choice in a city where meat-free dishes are a bit hard to find. Choose from crunchy salads, tasty soups, veggie pasta, and specials like tasty braised eggplant. *26 rue Montorgueil, 1st.* ☎ *01-40-13-02-53. Entrees 5€–14€; prix fixe 9€–13€. MC, V. Métro: Châtelet or Les Halles. Map p 102.*

*Chartier serves up classic French brasserie cuisine.*

In A Moveable Feast, a memoir of 1920s literary society, Ernest Hemingway called Closerie des Lilas "one of the best cafes in Paris."

★ **Iode** LES HALLES *SEAFOOD*
One of the city's best seafood restaurants draws crowds with its fresh fried shrimp; baked sea bass with a rich, creamy sauce; and tuna steak, grilled and served with sautéed vegetables. *48 rue d'Argout, 2nd.* ☎ *01-42-36-46-45. Entrees 14€–30€. MC, V. Lunch & dinner Mon–Fri; dinner Sat. Métro: Sentier. Map p 102.*

★★ **Jasmin** CHAILLOT *TRADITIONAL FRENCH* In a pale-green and pink dining room, chef Benoit Guichard knocks out classics like salmon tartare, filet of sole with oyster-cream sauce, and pigeon sausage with foie gras. *32 rue de Longchamp, 16th.* ☎ *01-45-53-00-07. Reservations far in advance. Entrees 45€–79€; prix fixe 50€ lunch, 95€ dinner. AE, DC, MC, V. Lunch & dinner Mon–Fri. Métro: Trocadéro. Map p 101.*

**La Poule au Pot** TUILERIES *TRADI-TIONAL FRENCH* This bistro welcomes late-night carousers and celebs like Mick Jagger and Prince for warm goat-cheese salad, onion soup, Burgundy-style escargot, and stewed chicken. Good fun. *9 rue Vauvilliers, 1st.* ☎ *01-42-36-32-96. Reservations recommended. Entrees*

20€–33€; prix fixe 30€. MC, V. Dinner Tues–Sun (until 5am). Métro: Louvre or Les Halles. Map p 102.

★★ **L'Astor** MADELEINE *MODERN FRENCH* Beneath an etched-glass Art Deco ceiling, talented chefs create fabulous dishes like caramelized sea urchins in aspic with fennel-flavored cream. But the food doesn't come cheap. *In the Hôtel Astor, 11 rue d'Astorg, 8th.* ☎ *01-53-05-05-20. Reservations required in advance,*

La Tour d'Argent offers a panoramic view of the Seine and Notre-Dame.

*Steak frites and omelets—staples of French bistro cuisine.*

especially for lunch. Entrees 60€–70€. AE, DC, MC, V. Lunch & dinner Mon–Fri; closed Aug. Métro: St-Augustin or Madeleine. Map p 101.

★★ **La Tour d'Argent** ST-GERMAIN-DES-PRES *TRADITIONAL FRENCH*   Dining at this penthouse restaurant is an event. The specialty of the house is the *caneton* (pressed duckling), as it has been since 1890, but I also recommend the pheasant consommé and pikeperch quenelles. *15–17 quai de la Tournelle, 5th.* ☎ *01-43-54-23-31. Reservations far in advance. Entrees 60€–70€; prix-fixe lunch 70€. AE, DC, MC, V. Lunch & dinner Wed–Sun; dinner Tues. Métro: St-Michel or Pont Marie. Map p 104.*

★ **Le Bistro de l'Etoile** PASSY *TRADITIONAL FRENCH*   This warm dining room serves affordable versions of grand cuisine, like sautéed scallops, rack of lamb *au jus,* and red snapper filet with caramelized endive. *19 rue Laruiston, 16th.* ☎ *01-40-67-11-16. Reservations recommended. Entrees 19€–26€; prix-fixe lunch 21€–26€. AE, DC, MC, V. Lunch Mon–Fri; dinner daily. Métro: Kléber. Map p 101.*

★★ **Le Dauphin** CONCORDE *SOUTHERN FRENCH*   This centrally located eatery is an excellent place to get a taste of southern-style French cooking, with dishes like rustic terrines, *lapereau* (rabbit), and stewed duck. *167 rue St-Honoré, 1st.* ☎ *01-42-60-40-11. Prix fixe 23€ lunch, 34€ dinner. AE, DC, MC, V. Lunch & dinner daily. Métro: Pyramides. Map p 102.*

★★★ **Le Grand Véfour** TUILERIES *TRADITIONAL FRENCH*   This romantic, historic, expensive place is a favorite of food critics. Specialties include lamb cooked with sweet wine, Breton lobster, and cabbage sorbet in dark-chocolate sauce. *17 rue de Beaujolais, 1st.* ☎ *01-42-96-56-27. Reservations far in advance. Entrees 65€–76€; prix fixe75€ lunch, 230€ dinner. AE, DC, MC, V. Lunch Mon–Fri; dinner Mon–Thurs. Closed Aug. Métro: Louvre-Palais Royal or Pyramides. Map p 102.*

★★ **Le Petit Flore** CONCORDE *TRADITIONAL FRENCH*   This excellent little restaurant offers tasty traditional French cuisine at very low prices. Dishes are simple (thin steaks with tomato salad, grilled fish with fried potatoes) but delicious. *6 rue Croix des Petits Champs, 1st.* ☎ *01-42-60-25-53. Prix fixe 12€. DC, MC, V. Métro: Palais Royal. Map p 102.*

**Le Petit Marché** MARAIS *TRADITIONAL FRENCH*   This place stays open late, and is popular with the nocturnal crowd. Food is unspectacular but satisfactory. Highlights of the menu include salads, steak pavé, fried fish, and stewed duck. *9 rue de Béarn, 3rd.* ☎ *01-42-72-06-67. Entrees 19€–25€. MC, V. Lunch & dinner daily. Closed Feb. Métro: St-Paul or Bastille. Map p 102.*

★★★ **Les Elysées du Vernet** MADELEINE *PROVENÇAL*   This restaurant is a gastronomic wonder.

*Les Elysées du Vernet's glass domed ceiling was designed by Gustav Eiffel.*

Enjoy imaginative dishes like shoulder of lamb with fruit compote, braised lobster with fresh rosemary, and fish-roe ravioli in a gorgeous dining room with a panoramic glass ceiling. *In the Hôtel Vernet, 25 rue Vernet, 8th.* ☎ *01-44-31-98-98. Reservations required well in advance. Entrees 42€–78€; menu gastronomique 115€. AE, DC, MC, V. Lunch & dinner Mon–Sat; dinner Sun. Métro: George-V. Map p 101.*

★ **Le Vieux Bistro** ILE DE LA CITE *TRADITIONAL FRENCH* With a great location right across from Notre-Dame, this place is certainly convenient. Happily, it's very good, too, with fabulous stewed chicken, steak frites, and a wine list strong on bordeaux. *14 rue du Cloître-Notre-Dame, 4th.* ☎ *01-43-54-18-95. Entrees 15€–25€. No credit cards. Lunch & dinner daily. Métro: Cité or St-Michel. Map p 102.*

★★ **Ma Bourgogne** MARAIS *TRADITIONAL FRENCH* Its breezy outdoor patio in the Marais's gorgeous place des Vosges makes this is a great place for a summer lunch of one of the excellent house salads or thin-sliced steak. If you prefer your beef very rare indeed, you're in luck—steak tartare is the house specialty. *19 place des Vosges, 4th.* ☎ *01-42-78-44-64. Entrees*

21€–28€. *No credit cards. Lunch & dinner daily. Métro: St-Paul or Bastille. Map p 102.*

**Mimosa** GRANDS BOULEVARDS *RURAL FRENCH* This is a good place for a hearty lunch of French home cooking (peppery chicken stew, tomato-based broths). It's particularly good for fans of offal, as it's known for its tripe sausage *(andouillette)* and black pudding. *44 rue d'Argout, 2nd.* ☎ *01-40-28-15-75. Prix fixe 12€, 14€. MC, V. Lunch Mon–Fri. Métro: Sentier. Map p 102.*

★★ **Piccolo Teatro** MARAIS *VEGETARIAN* With stone walls and low beams, this is a charming place for lunch or dinner. Try the salads, fresh soups, and baguette sandwiches. For dessert, there are lovely fruit tarts. *6 rue des Ecouffes, 4th.* ☎ *01-42-72-17-79. Entrees 9€–15€ lunch, 14€–19€ dinner; prix fixe 15€ lunch, 21€ dinner. AE, DC, MC, V. Lunch & dinner daily. Métro: St-Paul or Hôtel-de-Ville. Map p 102.*

★ **Pitchi Poi** MARAIS *JEWISH* This Jewish restaurant (with a pretty patio for warm nights) leans toward Eastern Europe with smoked herring, gefilte fish, chunky bagels, and dainty blinis. Imported vodkas are another house specialty, as are unusual Eastern European drinks

*A cozy table at Restaurant d'Hélène.*

like *tsvica* (potent Romanian plum brandy). *7 rue Caron, 4th. ☎ 01-42-77-46-15. www.pitchipoi. com. Entrees 9€–19€; Sun brunch 25€. AE, DC, MC, V. Lunch & dinner Mon–Sat; brunch Sun (noon–4pm). Métro: St-Paul. Map p 102.*

### ★★ Restaurant d'Hélène/ Salon d'Hélène ST-GERMAIN-DES-PRES SOUTHWESTERN FRENCH

Hélène d'Arroze, the most famous female chef in Paris, creates modern southwestern French cuisine at these two pricey eateries—the restaurant is more formal; the salon livelier. Try the foie gras with grilled apples, skate with lemon and capers, and salad of white beans and clams. *4 rue d'Assas, 6th. ☎ 01-42-22-00-11. Reservations required. Restaurant: prix fixe 150€–195€. Salon: prix-fixe lunch 61€; tapas 7€–15€. AE, MC, V. Lunch & dinner Tues–Sat. Métro: Sèvres-Babylone. Map p 104.*

### ★★★ Restaurant Plaza Athénée (Alain Ducasse)

MADELEINE *MODERN FRENCH* Five-star Michelin wonder-chef Alain Ducasse uses produce from around the country in mouthwatering dishes that range from Bresse fowl and cuttlefish to thick grilled pork. Superb wine list. *In the Plaza Athénée hotel, 25 av. Montaigne, 8th. ☎ 01-53-67-66-65. Reservations 6–8 weeks in advance. Entrees 70€–105€; prix fixe 190€–300€. AE, DC, MC, V. Lunch Thurs–Fri; dinner Mon–Fri. Closed mid-July to Aug. Métro: Alma-Marceau. Map p 101.*

### ★★★ Taillevent MADELEINE

*MODERN FRENCH* Occupying a 19th-century town house off the Champs-Elysées with paneled rooms and crystal chandeliers, this is widely known as the city's best restaurant. Try the sausage of Breton lobster, the watercress soup with Sevruga caviar, or the salmon in sea salt. *15 rue Lamennais, 8th. ☎ 01-44-95-15-01. Reservations 6 weeks in advance. Entrees 34€–90€; dégustation menu 130€. AE, DC, MC, V. Lunch & dinner Mon–Fri. Closed Aug. Métro: George-V. Map p 101.* ●

*Restaurant Plaza Athénée, home to star chef Alain Ducasse.*

# Nightlife Best Bets

Best **for Vodka Martinis—Shaken, Not Stirred**
★★★ Bar du Crillon *In the Hôtel de Crillon, 10 place de la Concorde* (p 121)

Best **Bar in Paris**
★★★ Bar Hemingway *In the Hôtel Ritz, 15 place Vendôme* (p 121)

Best **Happy Hour**
★ Bob Cool *15 rue de Grands Augustins* (p 121)

Best **Wine Bar**
★★ La Bacchantes *21 rue Caumartin* (p 120)

Best **Place for Journalists Looking for Friends**
★★ Willi's Wine Bar *13 rue des Petits-Champs* (p 120)

Best **for Students**
★ Académie de la Bière *88 bd. du Port Royal* (p 120)

Best **for Fans of Papa**
★★★ Harry's Bar *5 rue Daunou* (p 121)

Best **for Smoking Havana Cigars**
★★ Maito Habana *19 rue de Presbourg* (p 122)

Best **Celeb Hangout**
★★ Man Ray *34 rue Marbeuf* (p 122)

Best **for a Little Salsa Action**
Barrio Latino *46 rue du Faubourg St-Antoine* (p 123)

Best **Waterfront Location**
★★ Bateau Concorde Atlantique *Facing 25 quai Anatole-France* (p 123)

Best **for Doors Fans**
★★ Wagg *62 rue Mazarine* (p 124)

Best **for the Latest Techno Sounds**
★★ Rex *5 bd. Poissonniére* (p 123)

Best **Gay Bars**
Open Café & Café Cox *15 & 17 rue des Archives* (p 124)

Best **Lesbian Bar**
La Champmeslé *4 rue Chabanais* (p 124)

Best **for Those Over 30**
★★★ Le Bar de L'Hôtel *13 rue des Beaux-Arts* (p 122)

*Come to Le Pantalon to mix with a fun, international crowd.*

# Right Bank (8th & 16th–17th)

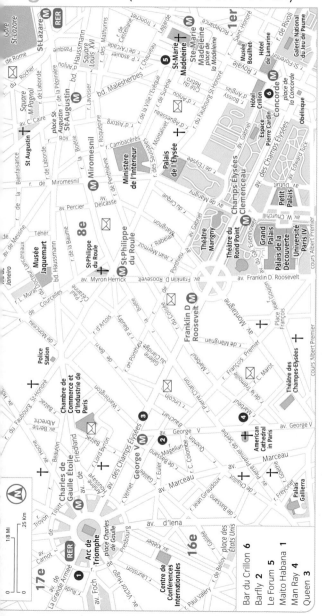

Bar du Crillon 6
Barfly 2
Le Forum 5
Maito Habana 1
Man Ray 4
Queen 3

# Right Bank (1st–4th & 9th–11th)

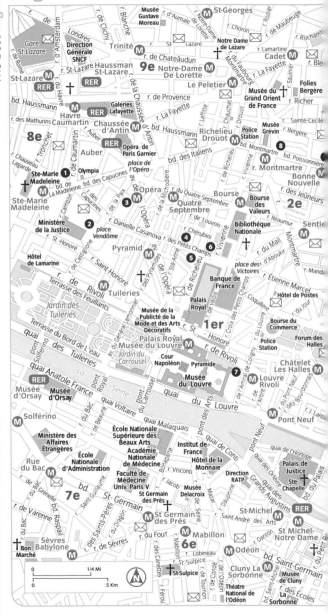

Aux Négociants **10**
Bar Hemingway **2**
Barrio Latino **16**
China Club **17**
Harry's Bar **3**
Juveniles **5**
La Bacchantes **1**
La Belle Hortense **14**
La Champmeslé **4**
La Tartine **15**
Le Fumoir **7**
Le Gibus **11**
Nouveau Casino **12**
Open Café/Café Cox **13**
Pulp **8**
Rex **9**
Willi's Wine Bar **6**

# Left Bank (5th–6th)

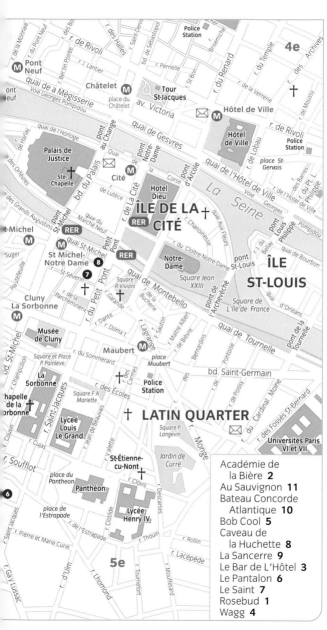

Académie de
la Bière **2**
Au Sauvignon **11**
Bateau Concorde
Atlantique **10**
Bob Cool **5**
Caveau de
la Huchette **8**
La Sancerre **9**
Le Bar de L'Hôtel **3**
Le Pantalon **6**
Le Saint **7**
Rosebud **1**
Wagg **4**

# Paris Nightlife A to Z

## Wine Bars

**★ Au Sauvignon** INVALIDES
This tiny bar, with ceramic tiles and colorful frescoes, has tables overflowing onto the terrace, where a cheerful crowd downs wines from the cheapest Beaujolais to the priciest Grand Cru. *80 rue des Sts-Pères, 7th.* ☎ *01-45-48-49-02. Métro: Sévres-Babylone. Map p 115.*

**★ Aux Négociants** MONTMARTRE
A quality Loire Valley wine list and reasonable prices draw everyone from artists to office workers to shopkeepers to this wine bar, a 10-minute walk downhill from the Sacré Coeur. *27 rue Lambert, 18th.* ☎ *Métro: Lamarck-Caulincourt or Château Rouge. Map p 118.*

**★ Juveniles** TUILERIES This sleek place prides itself on its enormous wine cellar with labels from around the world. The trendy crowd stays busy watching itself in the mirror. *47 rue des Richelieu, 1st.* ☎ *01-42-07-46-49. Métro: Palais Royal. Map p 116.*

**★★ La Bacchantes** MADELEINE
This place claims to offer more wines by the glass (at least 50) than any other bar in Paris, so don't come here if you're prone to indecision. Exposed beams and paneling add character, and chalkboards list special vintages and platters. *21 rue Caumartin, 9th.* ☎ *01-42-65-25-35. Métro: Opéra or Madeleine. Map p 116.*

**★ La Sancerre** INVALIDES This charmingly old-fashioned cafe has friendly staff and excellent Loire Valley wines, as well as a first-rate Pinot de Bourgogne (a burgundy). Lots of tasty food to nibble on as well. *22 av. Rapp, 7th.* ☎ *01-45-51-75-91. Métro: Alma-Marceau. Map p 118.*

**★ La Tartine** MARAIS With its mirrors, brass, and chandeliers, this place looks like a movie set. The wine list climbs beyond 50 varieties, including seven kinds of Beaujolais. *24 rue de Rivoli, 4th.* ☎ *01-42-72-76-85. Métro: St-Paul. Map p 116.*

**★★ Willi's Wine Bar** TUILERIES
A favorite of journalists and stockbrokers, this place in the city's financial district has a bit of an English touch, thanks to its expat owner. Still, it's all about wine, with 250 labels and plenty to try by the glass. *13 rue des Petits-Champs, 1st.* ☎ *01-42-61-05-09. Métro: Bourse, Pyramides, or Palais Royal. Map p 116.*

## Pubs & Bars

**★ Académie de la Bière** LATIN QUARTER The decor in this academy of beer is subdued enough, with a wood-paneled, rustic look,

*Pop open a bottle of bubbly or sample some bordeaux at one of Paris's many wine bars.*

but the mood can nonetheless be raucous. Most of the beers on tap come from Belgium. *88 bd. du Port Royal, 5th.* ☎ *01-43-54-66-65. Métro: Port Royal. Map p 118.*

★★★ **Bar du Crillon** CONCORDE This formal, elegant old bar played a role in Hemingway's *The Sun Also Rises.* Today, as then, its regulars include diplomats, heiresses, movie stars, and hangers-on. Expect to pay upwards of 8€ for a cocktail. *C'est la vie. In the Hôtel de Crillon, 10 place de la Concorde, 8th.* ☎ *01-44-71-15-00. Métro: Concorde. Map p 115.*

★★ **Barfly** MADELEINE Style counts for the hip crowd that frequents this artfully decorated bar and supper club, so dress up. Wood floors, photo-realist paintings and statues, and a long blue-stone bar make up the unique decor. The restaurant serves a late supper of Asian-fusion cuisine for 40€ a head. *49–51 av. George V, 8th.* ☎ *01-53-67-84-60. Métro: George-V Map p 115.*

★★★ **Bar Hemingway** VEN-DOME One of the best bars on earth has been commemorated in book, film, and song for more than half a century. In 1944, Hemingway and Allied soldiers famously liberated it from the Nazis and ordered a round of martinis. Today it's just as you might expect—book-filled, wood-paneled, and loaded with memorabilia. Expect well-mixed drinks, an excellent staff, and high prices. *In the Hôtel Ritz, 15 place Vendôme, 1st.* ☎ *01-43-16-30-30. Métro: Opéra. Map p 116.*

★ **Bob Cool** ST-GERMAIN-DES-PRES The hip and the laid-back vie for your attention at this trendy bar that's a magnet for writers and artists and lots of very pretty people of all persuasions. It's worth showing up for happy hour (5–9pm) just to see the mayhem.*15 rue de Grands Augustins,* *6th.* ☎ *01-46-33-33-77. Métro: Odéon or St-Michel. Map p 118.*

**China Club** BASTILLE Polish your cheekbones before heading out to this club, popular with Paris's fashion world. Downstairs looks like a crowded Shanghai brothel circa 1930, while upstairs is a bit more decorous and less over the top. A Chinese restaurant on the ground floor will fill you up when it gets late. *50 rue de Charenton, 12th.* ☎ *01-43-43-82-02. Métro: Bastille or Ledru Rollin. Map p 118.*

★★★ **Harry's Bar** TUILERIES This place is sacred to Hemingway disciples as the place where he and the rest of the ambulance corps drank themselves silly during the Spanish Civil War. This bar is responsible for the White Lady and the Sidecar, along with numerous damaged livers. A pianist plays in the cellar; upstairs is vaguely more sophisticated. Filled with expats, this place is more fun than you might think. *5 rue Daunou, 2nd.* ☎ *01-42-61-71-14. Métro: Opéra or Pyramides. Map p 116.*

*Classy Bar Hemingway boasts some of the best bartenders in the city.*

**La Belle Hortense** MARAIS
The fact that this quirky bar has a bookshop within its walls makes it a perpetual favorite of my bookish Parisian friends. The crowd of regulars can discuss the finer points of Gertrude Stein at the drop of a *château*. Casual and clever. *13 vieille du Temple, 4th.* ☎ *01-48-04-71-60. Métro: Hôtel-de-Ville. Map p 116.*

★★★ **Le Bar de L'Hôtel** ST-GERMAIN-DES-PRES This place is appropriately theatrical (lots of marble, a Victorian color scheme, and baroque touches) when you consider that its regulars tend to be in the film industry—or want to be. When you take into account that this was the hotel where Oscar Wilde died, impoverished and abandoned, it takes on a kind of poignancy. It's a lovely historic place for a drink and a ponder. *13 rue des Beaux-Arts, 6th.* ☎ *01-44-41-99-00. Métro: St-Germain-des-Prés. Map p 118.*

★ **Le Forum** MADELEINE This business-crowd favorite is like a London private club—all oak paneling, single-malts, and brass. Try a champagne cocktail and soak up the atmosphere. *4 bd. Malesherbes, 8th.* ☎ *01-42-65-37-86. Métro: Madeleine. Map p 115.*

★★ **Le Fumoir** TUILERIES Well-paid, well-educated, well-lubricated locals keep this place hopping Friday nights. It has the look of an English library; 6,000 books provide a worthy backdrop for the festivities. There's a decent international menu, should you get the munchies. *6 rue de l'Admiral de Coligny, 1st.* ☎ *01-42-92-00-24. Métro: Louvre-Rivoli. Map p 116.*

★★ **Le Pantalon** LATIN QUARTER This unusual-looking place, with quirky sculpture and dizzying ladies' rooms, not to mention its crazy crew of regulars, makes for a ridiculously fun night out. It draws an international crowd, but with an emphasis firmly on French. *7 rue Royer-Collard, 5th. No phone. RER: Luxembourg. Map p 118.*

★★ **Maito Habana** PASSY The masculine brown-and-green decor smacks of a men's club, as do the smell of cigars, glasses of Scotch, and, well, all the men. Enjoy a Cuban cigar and a cocktail. Bands play at 11pm. *19 rue de Presbourg, 16th.* ☎ *01-45-00-84-84. Métro: Etoile. Map p 115.*

★★ **Man Ray** MADELEINE Photographs taken by this sleek bar's namesake cover its walls. Given that it's owned by Johnny Depp, Sean Penn, and John Malkovich, it should come as no surprise that it's discreet, eclectic, pricey, and popular with international celebs. *34 rue Marbeuf, 8th.* ☎ *01-56-88-36-36. Cover 15€ (after 11pm Fri only). Métro: Franklin-D.-Roosevelt. Map p 115.*

*Paris nightclubs draw some of Europe's best DJs.*

**★★ Rosebud** DENFERT   The popularity of this place, known for a bemused and indulgent attitude toward anyone looking for a drink and some conversation, hasn't diminished over the decades. The crowd is generally over 30, clever, pleasant, and tipsy. Food is U.S.-based and reasonably priced. *11 bis rue Delambre, 14th.* ☎ *01-43-35-38-54. Métro: Vavin. Map p 118.*

## Dance Clubs

**Barrio Latino** BASTILLE   Fans of Latin music and Parisian charm fall for this place every time. The huge building holds tapas bars, dance floors, a Latin restaurant, and a private VIP lounge. The staff rolls tapas-loaded carts around. The dancing at street level is hot. Try a Cuba Libre and join in. *46 rue du Faubourg St-Antoine, 12th.* ☎ *01-55-78-84-75. Cover 8€ Fri–Sat. Métro: Bastille. Map p 116.*

**★★ Bateau Concorde Atlantique** INVALIDES   This boat-based nightspot keeps clubbers afloat in summer with a cool, waterfront terrace and huge dance floor. A unique place to party. *Facing 25 quai Anatole-France, 7th.* ☎ *01-47-05-71-03. Cover 10€–15€. Métro: Assemblée Nationale. Map p 118.*

**Caveau de la Huchette** LATIN QUARTER   This rocking club has an emphasis on good times, partying, and loud music. The crowd tends to be in their 30s and above, with a backdrop of funk, jazz, and classic rock. *5 rue de la Huchette, 5th.* ☎ *01-43-26-65-05. Cover 10€–13€. Métro: St-Michel. Map p 118.*

**Le Saint** LATIN QUARTER   This happening club packs in the young and energetic for nightly jams to French and international hip-hop, disco, and funk. Come ready to dance. *7 rue St-Séverin, 5th.*

☎ *01-43-25-50-04. Cover 15€. Métro: St-Michel. Map p 118.*

**★★ Nouveau Casino** REPUBLIQUE   This is one of the city's hottest clubs from Wednesday to Saturday, when local collectives and international names take over the DJ booth. From club to techno with stop-offs at jungle, it's a good place to see how the French get down. *102 rue Oberkamph, 11th.* ☎ *01-43-57-57-40. Cover 7€–15€. Métro: Parmentier. Map p 116.*

**Queen** BOURSE   Once a gay club (which explains the name), this very-late-night club attracts a mixed crowd of corporate workers kicking back, ladies out for a night of dancing, and tourists in the know. Occasionally attracts international DJs. *102 av. des Champs-Elysées, 8th.* ☎ *01-53-89-08-90. www.queen.fr. Cover 10€–20€. Métro: George-V. Map p 115.*

**★★ Rex** BOURSE   This place is known for its cutting-edge electronic music, with top DJs playing weekly, and frequent free nights. Check local listings to see who's at the helm. *5 bd. Poissonniére, 2nd.* ☎ *01-42-36-10-96. Cover up to 16€. Métro: Bonne Nouvelle. Map p 116.*

*A 1950s theme night at Caveau de la Huchette.*

*The crowds at Open Café and Café Cox often spill out onto the street.*

★★ **Wagg** PALAIS LUXEMBOURG This was once the Whisky Go Go, a favorite of Jim Morrison during his last days. Now it's owned by the people behind London's Fabric club, and it lures techno-holics from around the world. *62 rue Mazarine, 6th.* ☎ *01-55-42-22-00. Cover 5€– 12€. Métro: Odéon. Map p 118.*

**Gay & Lesbian Bars & Clubs**
**La Champmeslé** TUILERIES Dim lighting, background music, and banquets set the scene at this cozy meeting place for lesbians. The 300-year-old building features exposed stone, ceiling beams, and 1950s-style furnishing. There's a cabaret every Thursday and Saturday at 10pm, and art exhibits every month. *4 rue Chabanais, 2nd.* ☎ *01-42-96-85-20. Métro: Pyramides or Bourse. Map p 116.*

**Le Gibus** REPUBLIQUE This late-night club entertains diverse groups throughout the week, and mostly gay men on weekends, when drag shows sometimes form part of the entertainment. *18 rue du Faubourg du Temple, 11th.* ☎ *01-47-00-78-88. Cover 18€ Fri–Sat. Métro: République. Map p 116.*

**Open Café & Café Cox** MARAIS This pair of gay men's bars are two independent businesses, but there's so much traffic between them they're often thought of as a single place. You'll find the most mixed gay crowd in Paris here. *15 & 17 rue des Archives, 4th.* ☎ *01-42-72-26-18 & 01-42-72-08-00. Métro: Hôtel-de-Ville. Map p 116.*

**Pulp** GRANDS BOULEVARDS This popular lesbian dance club looks like a 19th-century French music hall. It attracts a mixed crowd on Wednesday and Thursday. International DJs keep things hopping. *25 bd. Poissonnière, 2nd.* ☎ *01-40-26-01-93. Cover 12€ Fri–Sat. Métro: Grands Boulevards. Map p 116.* ●

# Arts & Entertainment Best Bet

Best **Opera House**
★★★ Opéra Bastille, *2 place de la Bastille* (p 132)

Best **Place to Walk in the Phantom's Footsteps**
★★★ Opéra Garnier, *place de l'Opéra* (p 132)

Best **Concert Hall**
★★★ Olympia, *28 bd. des Capucines* (p 132)

Best **Place to Hear Classical Music**
Théâtre des Champs-Elysées, *15 av. Montaigne* (p 132)

Best **Theater**
★ Comédie Française, *2 rue de Richelieu* (p 132)

Best **Drag Show**
Chez Michou, *80 rue des Martyrs* (p 134)

Best **Place to Learn Old French Drinking Songs**
★ Au Lapin Agile, *22 rue des Saules* (p 134)

Best **Place to Try Absinthe**
★ Moulin Rouge, *place Blanche* (p 135)

Best **Cabaret**
★★ Lido de Paris, *116 bis av. des Champs-Elysées* (p 135)

Best **Place for 20-Somethings**
★ Caveau de la Huchette, *5 rue de la Huchette* (p 135)

Best **Place to See & be Seen**
★ New Morning, *7–9 rue des Petites-Ecuries* (p 136)

Best **Overall Jazz Club**
★★★ Le Bilboquet, *13 rue St-Benoît* (p 135)

Best **Nouvelle Orleans Jazz**
★★★ Slow Club, *130 rue de Rivoli* (p 136)

Best **Free Show**
The Show, *Ile de la Cité* (p 136)

*Neon lights up the windmill on top of the Moulin Rouge.*

# Right Bank (8th & 18th)

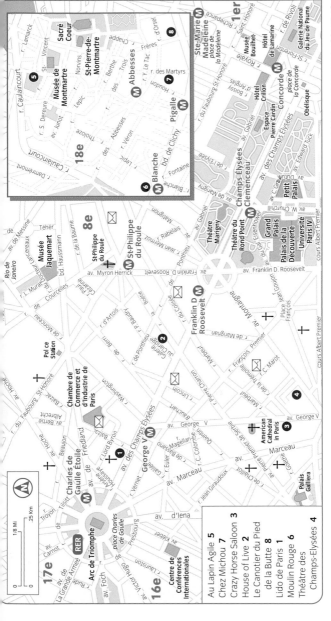

Au Lapin Agile 5
Chez Michou 7
Crazy Horse Saloon 3
House of Live 2
Le Canotier du Pied
de la Butte 8
Lido de Paris 1
Moulin Rouge 6
Théâtre des
Champs-Elysées 4

The Best Arts & Entertainment

# Right Bank (1st–4th & 9th–11th)

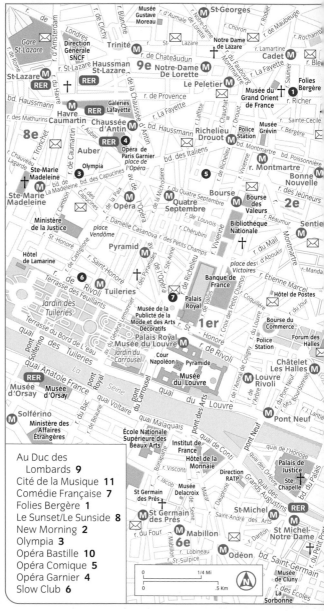

Au Duc des
  Lombards 9
Cité de la Musique 11
Comédie Française 7
Folies Bergère 1
Le Sunset/Le Sunside 8
New Morning 2
Olympia 3
Opéra Bastille 10
Opéra Comique 5
Opéra Garnier 4
Slow Club 6

The Best Arts & Entertainment

# Left Bank (5th–6th)

Au Caveau de la Bolée **3**
Caveau de la Huchette **4**
L'Arbuci **2**
Le Bilboquet **1**
Le Paradis Latin **6**
Le Who's Bar **5**

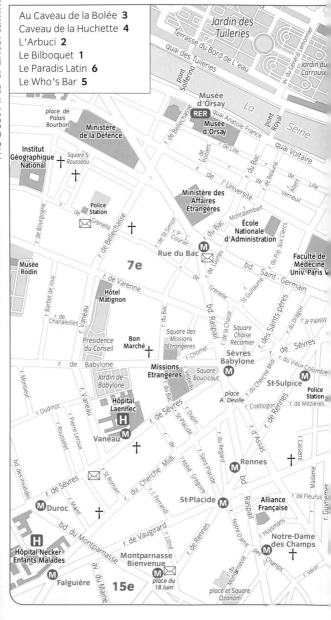

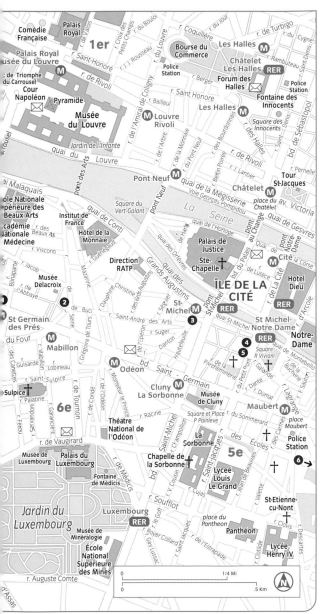

Comédie Française
Palais Royal
Palais Royal usée du Louvre
: de Triomphe du Carrousel
Cour Napoléon
Pyramide
Musée du Louvre
r. Saint-Honoré
r. de Rivoli
Jardin de l'Infante
quai du Louvre

**1er**

r. Croix des Petits Champs
r. du Bouloi
r. J.J. Rousseau
r. du Louvre
r. Coquillière
r. du Jour
r. de Turbigo
r. du Cygne

Bourse du Commerce
Les Halles
Châtelet Les Halles
r. Rambuteau
Saint-Denis

Police Station
r. Berger
r. Saint Honore
Forum des Halles
Les Halles

Fontaine des Innocents
Square des Innocents
r. des Halles
bd. de Sébastopol

r. de l'Amiral de Coligny
r. de Bailleul
r. de l'Arbre
r. de la Monnaie
r. du Pont Neuf
r. des Bourdonnais
r. Betin Porrée
r. J. Lantier
r. de Rivoli
r. Pernelle

Louvre Rivoli

Tour St-Jacques

quai de la Mégisserie
Voie Georges Pompidou
Pont Neuf
quai de l'Horloge
Châtelet
place du av. Victoria
Châtelet

La Seine
quai de Gesvres

ai Malaquais
ole Nationale périeure des Beaux Arts
cadémie r. des lationale Beaux Ar Médecine
r. Visconti

Square du Vert-Galant
Institut de France
Hôtel de la Monnaie
Direction RATP

quai de Conti
quai des Grands Augustins
quai des Orfèvres
quai des Grands Augustins

La Corse
quai de la Cité
quai du Marché
quai de l'Horloge
pont au Change
Quai de
Cité
pont Notre-Dame

Palais de Justice
Ste-Chapelle

**ÎLE DE LA CITÉ**

r. Bonaparte
r. Jacob
r. de l'Abbaye
Musée Delacroix

Mazarine
r. Guénégaud
r. Dauphine
r. Christine
r. des Grands Augustins
r. Séguier
St-Michel
St-André des Arts

Hotel Dieu

quai du Palais
r. de Lutèce
Cité
de La Cité
r. d'Arcole

St Germain des Prés
du Four

r. de Buci
r. de Seine
r. Saint-André des Arts
r. Suger
r. de l'Eperon
r. Danton
quai St-Michel

St Michel Notre Dame

Notre-Dame

Mabillon
des Canettes
r. Guisarde
r. Mabillon
Lobineau
r. Grégoire de Tours

Odéon

bd. Saint Germain
r. Hautefeuille
r. de la Parcheminerie
r. du Petit Pont
r. Galande
r. Dante
r. Dumat
r. Lagrange
quai de Montebello
de la Bucherie
r. F.F. Sauton

Square R Viviani

t-Sulpice
r. Palatine
r. Férou

**6e**

r. Monsieur le Prince
r. de Condé
r. de l'Odéon
r. de Tournon
r. Racine

Cluny La Sorbonne
Musée de Cluny
Square et Place P Painlevé
r. du Sommerard

Maubert
place Maubert
des Carmes
des Ecoles

Police Station

r. de Vaugirard
r. de Médicis

Théâtre National de l'Odéon

Saint-Michel
bd. St-Michel
r. Champollion
r. V. Cousin
r. Cujas
Chapelle de la Sorbonne

La Sorbonne
Lycée Louis Le Grand

r. Saint-Jacques
r. Jean de Beauvais
r. de Lanneau
r. Valette

**5e**

St-Etienne-cu-Nont
r. Clovis
r. Clotilde
r. Descartes

Musée de Luxembourg
Palais du Luxembourg
Fontaine de Médicis

Luxembourg

r. Soufflot
place du Panthéon
Panthéon
Lycée Henry IV

**Jardin du Luxembourg**

Musée de Minéralogie
École National Supérieure des Mines
r. Auguste Comte
d'Assas

r. Le Goff
r. Royer Collard
r. Gay Lussac
r. Saint Jacques
r. de l'Estrapade

0      1/4 Mi
0                .5 Km

# Arts & Entertainment **A to Z**

*Crowds gather for a performance at the Opéra Bastille.*

### Theater
★ **Comédie Française** TUILERIES
Those with even a modest understanding of French will enjoy a sparkling production at this national theater, where the main goal is to keep the classics alive while promoting contemporary authors. *2 rue de Richelieu, 1st.* ☎ *01-44-58-15-15. Tickets 20€–30€. Métro: Palais Royal–Musée du Louvre. Map p 128.*

### Opera, Dance & Classical
★ **Cité de la Musique**
BELLEVILLE This multimillion-euro structure incorporates a network of concert halls, libraries, and music research centers. It hosts a variety of concerts from Renaissance music to modern works. *221 av. Jean Jaurès, 19th.* ☎ *01-44-84-45-00. Tickets 6.50€–12€. Métro: Porte de Pantin. Map p 128.*

★★★ **Opéra Bastille** BASTILLE
This huge, contemporary building hosts outstanding opera performances, like Mozart's *Marriage of Figaro* and Tchaikovsky's *Queen of Spades,* in its three concert halls. Symphony and dance performances are held here as well. *2 place de la Bastille, 4th.* ☎ *01-40-01-17-89. Tickets 20€–114€ (opera); 20€–80€ (dance). Métro: Bastille. Map p 128.*

★★ **Opéra Comique** BOURSE
This is a charming venue for light opera on a smaller scale than the city's major opera houses. Built in the 1980s, it's a lovely place to see *Carmen, Don Giovanni,* or *Tosca. 5 rue Favart, 2nd.* ☎ *08-25-00-00-58. Closed mid-July to mid-Aug. Tickets 15€–100€. Métro: Richelieu-Drouot. Map p 128.*

★★★ **Opéra Garnier** OPERA
The phantom did his haunting here when it was a premier opera venue; now it's home to the city's ballet scene, although it still hosts opera from time to time. The 1875 building is a rococo wonder. *Place de l'Opéra, 9th.* ☎ *01-40-01-17-89. Tickets 23€–114€ (opera); 9€–70€ (dance). Métro: Opéra. Map p 128.*

**Théâtre des Champs-Elysées**
MADELEINE National and international orchestras (such as the Vienna Philharmonic) fill this Art Deco theater with sound, to the delight of its well-dressed audiences. *15 av. Montaigne, 8th.* ☎ *01-49-52-50-50. Tickets 10€–114€. Métro: Alma-Marceau. Map p 127.*

### A Music Hall
★★★ **Olympia** OPERA An eclectic series of local and international musicians, rock groups, acrobats, and

# Buying Tickets

The easiest (and most expensive) way to get tickets, especially if you're staying in a first-class or deluxe hotel, is to ask your concierge to arrange for them. A service fee is added, but it's a lot easier if you don't want to waste precious hours in Paris trying to secure hard-to-get tickets.

There are many ticket agencies in Paris, most near the Right Bank hotels. Avoid them if possible. You can buy the cheapest tickets at the box office of the theater or at discount agencies that sell tickets at discounts of up to 50%. One is the **Kiosque Théâtre,** 15 place de la Madeleine, 8th (no phone; Métro: Madeleine), offering leftover tickets at about half-price on performance day. Tickets for evening shows are sold Tuesday to Friday from 12:30 to 8pm and Saturday from 2 to 8pm. Tickets for matinees are sold Saturday from 12:30 to 2pm and Sunday from 12.30 to 4pm. Students with ID can often get last-minute tickets by applying at the box office an hour before curtain time.

If you'd like to buy tickets before you go, check with **Keith Prowse** (www.keithprowse.com). The company will mail tickets to you, or leave tickets at the box office for pickup prior to the performance. There's a markup of about 25% over box-office prices on each ticket, which includes handling charges. Keith Prowse sells to customers all over the world, including the United States, Canada, the United Kingdom, Australia, and New Zealand.

*Elaborate embellishments and sculptures grace the facade of the Opéra Garnier.*

comedians fill this famed old hall. You might catch all of them on the same night, if you're lucky. *28 bd. des Capucines, 9th.* ☎ *01-92-68-33-68. Tickets 30€–60€. Métro: Opéra or Madeleine. Map p 128.*

### Music Clubs & Cabarets
### ★★ Au Caveau de la Bolée

LATIN QUARTER   This raucous little music club is in the catacombs of a 14th-century abbey, and thus has a wonderful Parisian atmosphere. The singing is loud and the lyrics naughty, to the delight of the young, inebriated crowd. Magic acts also entertain. *25 rue de l'Hirondelle, 6th.* ☎ *01-43-54-62-20. Cover 50€ with dinner; 25€ without dinner. Métro: St-Michel. Map p 130.*

*Au Lapin Agile.*

★ **Au Lapin Agile** MONTMARTRE
This little cottage was a favorite of
Picasso when it was known as the
Cabaret des Assassins. Today it's a
dimly lit, memorabilia-filled place
where the crowd sings along to
French folk tunes and sea chanties.
*22 rue des Saules, 18th.* ☎ *01-46-
06-85-87. Cover (including 1 drink)
24€. Métro: Lamarck-Caulaincourt.
Map p 127.*

**Chez Michou** PIGALLE This
eccentric place is run by a veteran
impresario whose 20 cross-dressing
belles lip-sync Whitney Houston and
Mireille Mathieu while wearing
bizarre costumes. If you don't have
dinner, you must stand at the bar
and pay a compulsory 31€ for your
first drink. *80 rue des Martyrs, 18th.*
☎ *01-46-06-16-04. Cover (including
dinner, aperitif, wine, coffee & show)
95€. Métro: Pigalle. Map p 127.*

★ **Crazy Horse Saloon**
MADELEINE This sophisticated strip
joint thrives on its—ahem—good
choreography, or so its regulars
(mostly businessmen) say. Basically,
it's a sophisticated take on the usual
sex show. *12 av. George-V, 8th.*
☎ *01-47-23-32-32. Reservations recommended. Cover 69€–90€ (including 2 drinks); with dinner 125€–155€.
Métro: George-V or Alma-Marceau.
Map p 127.*

★ **Folies Bergère** GRANDS
BOULEVARDS An institution since
1869, this is where Josephine Baker
became the toast of Paris. But this is
not the wink-nudge place of the past.
Now it's a conventional theater with
a roster of musicals in French. *34
rue Richer, 9th.* ☎ *01-44-79-98-98.
Tickets 32€–52€; with dinner 90€.
Métro: Grands Boulevards or Cadet.
Map p 128.*

**Le Canotier du Pied de la
Butte** MONTMARTRE This cabaret,
popular with tourists, features performances in which two men and two
women trade jokes and sing popular
French songs by Piaf, Montand, Brel,
and Chevalier. Nostalgia is the theme.
*62 bd. Rochechouart, 18th.* ☎ *01-46-
06-02-86. Reservations required.
Cover 38€, including 1 drink. Métro:
Anvers. Map p 127.*

★ **Le Paradis Latin** LATIN QUAR-
TER Built by Alexandre-Gustave
Eiffel, this club introduced vaudeville
to Paris in the 19th century. Today its
colorful performances, with singers,
dancers, and special effects, hearken
back to that time. Expect some top-
lessness. *28 rue Cardinal Lemoine,
5th.* ☎ *01-43-25-28-28. Cover 75€
including champagne; 109€–200€
with dinner. Métro: Jussieu or Cardinal Lemoine. Map p 130.*

## ★★ Lido de Paris MADELEINE
This glossy club puts on multimillion-euro performances in a dramatic reworking of the classic Parisian cabaret shows, with special effects including aerial and aquatic ballets—even an occasional ice rink. *116 bis av. des Champs-Elysées, 8th. ☎ 800/227-4884 in the U.S., or 01-40-76-56-10. Dinner dance 140€–200€; show only 100€. Prices include half a bottle of champagne per person. Métro: George-V. Map p 127.*

## ★ Moulin Rouge MONTMARTRE
Toulouse-Lautrec immortalized this windmill-topped building and its scantily clad cancan dancers. Today it's true to its original theme of strip routines and sex. Expect tacky and tawdry, and you won't be disappointed. *Place Blanche, 18th. ☎ 01-53-09-82-82. Cover 82€–92€ including champagne; dinner & show 130€–160€; seats at bar 63€. Métro: Blanche. Map p 127.*

## Jazz, Rock & More
Au Duc des Lombards CONCORDE This thriving jazz club features performances nightly that range in style from free jazz to hard bop. Tables can be reserved. *42 rue des Lombards, 1st. ☎ 01-42-33-22-88. Cover 19€. Métro: Châtelet. Map p 128.*

## ★ Caveau de la Huchette LATIN
QUARTER This celebrated jazz cave draws a young crowd, mostly university students, who dance to the music of well-known jazz combos. Robespierre hung out here in his time, so you can tell everyone you're here for the history. *5 rue de la Huchette, 5th. ☎ 01-43-26-65-05. Cover 11€ Sun–Thurs; 13€ Fri–Sat. Métro: Map p 130.*

House of Live CONCORDE This big music bar is a very popular place for young Parisians to take in roots, blues, and rock bands, most of them French or French-speaking, some infinitely better than others. Check for flyers to see who's playing this week. *124 rue La Boétie, 8th. ☎ 01-42-25-18-06. Cover 8€–15€. Métro: Franklin-D.-Roosevelt. Map p 127.*

## ★ L'Arbuci ST-GERMAIN-DES-PRES
This smoky, dimly lit, and artfully chaotic place is primarily a restaurant, but it offers jazz performances 5 days a week (Thurs–Sat at midnight). The music spans the jazz globe, and the mood is subdued. *25 rue de Buci, 6th. ☎ 01-44-32-16-00. No cover. Prix-fixe menu 15€–30€. Bar open until 3am. Métro: Mabillon or St-Germain-des-Prés. Map p 130.*

## ★★★ Le Bilboquet ST-GERMAIN-
DES-PRES The film *Paris Blues* was based here, and for good reason—this is one of the city's best jazz bars. The restaurant is wood-paneled with a copper ceiling and a sunken bar, and the music is outstanding. *13 rue St-Benoît, 6th. ☎ 01-45-48-81-84. No cover. Métro: St-Germain-des-Prés. Map p 130.*

Le Who's Bar LATIN QUARTER This gritty bar is where the latest Paris bands pay their dues. You never know who will be on stage,

*Paris is heaven for jazz lovers, who can choose from many high-quality venues.*

# Best Free Shows in Paris

On a warm Paris night, the best entertainment is often free. In the summer months, the area at the southeastern tip of Ile de la Cité, behind the Notre-Dame, becomes a stage of sorts for what is known simply as **"The Show."** This is a kind of Gallic version of the Sundowner Festival in Florida's Key West, in that, around sunset, performance artists, musicians, jugglers, mimes, and magicians all put on a show against the backdrop of the cathedral, turned golden in the evening light. The atmosphere is euphoric, the performances *can* be brilliant, and it makes for wonderful memories.

A later option is a stroll along the Seine after 10pm. From the pont de Sully, take a graveled pathway down on the Left Bank and turn right, away from Notre-Dame. As you stroll, you'll pass musicians and other performers, and when the music is good, spontaneous dance parties often break out. You'll have lots of young Parisians keeping you company.

and whether they'll be doing their own songs or covering Coldplay . . . again. The place is friendly enough, and the cover is affordable. *13 rue du Petit-Pont, 5th.* ☎ *01-43-54-80-71. Cover 7€–15€. Métro: St-Michel. Map p 130.*

★ **New Morning** EASTERN PARIS Jazz fanatics pack this respected club to drink, talk, and dance, not to mention check each other out—this is one of the city's "it" places to see and be seen. Celebs like Spike Lee and Prince have been spotted here. The club is popular with African and European musicians. *7–9 rue des Petites-Ecuries, 10th.* ☎ *01-45-23-51-41. www.new morning.com. Cover 16€–25€. Métro: Château d'Eau. Map p 128.*

★★★ **Slow Club** CONCORDE This is one of the most famous jazz cellars in Europe, set in medieval vaults that create marvelous acoustics. The emphasis is on New Orleans jazz, and the audience is well educated about the genre. *130 rue de Rivoli, 1st.* ☎ *01-42-33-84-30. Cover 13€. Métro: Châtelet. Map p 128.*

**Le Sunset/Le Sunside** CON-CORDE This staple of the Parisian jazz circuit is two bars in one, with separate jazz shows going on simultaneously. The look is minimalist, and artists are both European and U.S.-based. Le Sunside favors classic jazz, and Le Sunset goes for electric jazz and world music. Take your pick. *60 rue des Lombards, 1st.* ☎ *01-40-26-46-60. Cover 15€–20€. Métro: Châtelet. Map p 128.* ●

*Slow Club has live music every night but Wednesday.*

# **Lodging** Best Bets

Best **Views**
Hôtel Ermitage $ 24 rue Lamarck
(p 147)

Best **for Romantics**
★ Hôtel Duc de St-Simon $$$
14 rue de St-Simon (p 147)

Best **Historic Hotel**
Hôtel Abbatial St-Germain $$
46 bd. St-Germain (p 145)

Best **Boutique Hotel**
★ L'Hôtel $$$$ 13 rue des Beaux-
Arts (p 150)

Best **Kid-Friendly Hotel**
Timhôtel Le Louvre $$ 4 rue Croix
des Petits-Champs (p 150)

Best **Budget Hotel**
★ Hôtel Saintonge $$ 16 rue Saintonge (p 149)

Best **Luxury Hotel**
★★★ Hôtel Ritz $$$$$ 15 place
Vendôme (p 148)

Best **21st-Century Luxury**
★★★ Park Hyatt Vendôme $$$$$
3–5 rue de la Paix (p 150)

Best **Celebrity Spotting**
★★ Hôtel de Lutèce $$ 65 rue
St-Louis-en-l'Ile (p 146)

Best **for Film Buffs**
Hôtel du 7th Art $ 20 rue St-Paul
(p 147)

Best **Small Hotel**
★ Pavillon de Paris $$$ 7 rue de
Parme (p 150)

Best **for Literary Types**
★ Hotel Lenox $$ 9 rue de l'Univer-
sité (p 148)

Best **for Afternoons in the
Park**
★★ Hôtel Luxembourg Parc
$$$–$$$$ 42 rue de Vaugirad
(p 148)

Best **for Minimalists**
★ Hotel Bel-Ami $$$–$$$$
7–11 rue St-Benoit (p 145)

Best **for Jazz Lovers**
Le Petit Châtelet $ 9 rue St-Denis
(p 150)

*The Park Hyatt Vendôme's 19th-century exterior houses luxurious, contemporary guest rooms.*

# Right Bank (8th & 16th–18th)

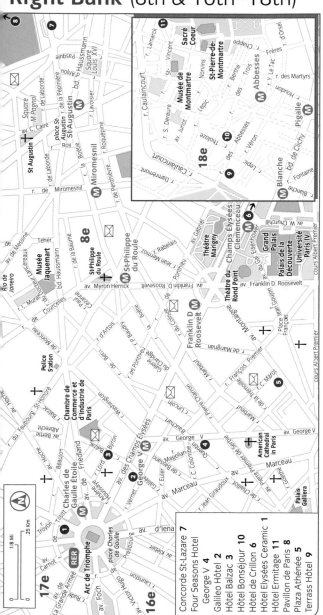

Concorde St-Lazare Hotel **7**
Four Seasons Hotel
George V **4**
Galileo Hôtel **2**
Hôtel Balzac **3**
Hôtel Bonséjour **10**
Hôtel de Crillon **6**
Hôtel Elysées Ceramic **1**
Hôtel Ermitage **11**
Pavillon de Paris **8**
Plaza Athénée **5**
Terrass Hôtel **9**

# Right Bank (1st–4th & 9th–11th)

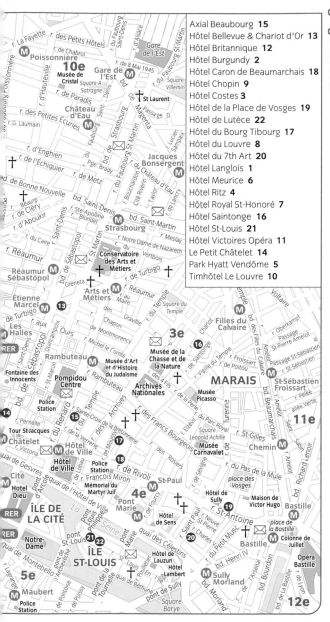

Axial Beaubourg **15**
Hôtel Bellevue & Chariot d'Or **13**
Hôtel Britannique **12**
Hôtel Burgundy **2**
Hôtel Caron de Beaumarchais **18**
Hôtel Chopin **9**
Hôtel Costes **3**
Hôtel de la Place de Vosges **19**
Hôtel de Lutèce **22**
Hôtel du Bourg Tibourg **17**
Hôtel du Louvre **8**
Hôtel du 7th Art **20**
Hôtel Langlois **1**
Hôtel Meurice **6**
Hôtel Ritz **4**
Hôtel Royal St-Honoré **7**
Hôtel Saintonge **16**
Hôtel St-Louis **21**
Hôtel Victoires Opéra **11**
Le Petit Châtelet **14**
Park Hyatt Vendôme **5**
Timhôtel Le Louvre **10**

# Left Bank (5th–6th)

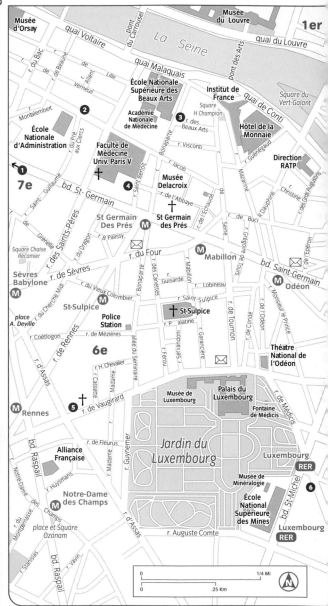

Musée
du Louvre

1er

Musée
d'Orsay

quai Voltaire

quai du Louvre

pont du Carrousel

La Seine

r. du Bac

de

de Beaune

Allent

quai Malaquais

pont des Arts

Lille

Verneuil

École Nationale
Supérieure des
Beaux Arts

Institut de
France

quai de Conti

Square du
Vert-Galant

Montalembert

2

Académie
Nationale
de Médecine

Square
H Champion

r. des
Beaux Arts

3

Bonaparte

Hôtel de la
Monnaie

École
Nationale
d'Administration

r. du Pré
aux Clercs

Faculté de
Médecine
Univ. Paris V

r. Visconti

r. Jacob

Mazarine

Guénégaud

Direction
RATP

1

7e

Saint-Guillaume

bd. St-Germain

Saint Benoît

Musée
Delacroix

r. de l'Abbaye

Nesle

Seine

r. de l'Échaudé

R. Dauphine

r.
Christine

r. des Grds Augustins

de

de Grenelle

du Dragon

r. B Palissy

St Germain
Des Prés

M

St Germain
des Prés

r. de Buci

r. Grégoire de Tours

bd. Saint-Germain

r. de l'Éperon

Square Chaise
Récamier

r. des Saints-Pères

r. du Four

r. des Canettes

r.
Guisarde

Mabillon

M

Sèvres
Babylone

M

r. de Sèvres

r. du Vieux Colombier

r. Mabillon

r. Lobineau

Odéon

M

du Cherche Midi

St-Sulpice

M

r. Bonaparte

r. Saint-Sulpice

r. de Tournon

r. de Condé

r. de l'Odéon

Monsieur le Prince

place
A. Deville

r. Coëtlogon

de Rennes

Police
Station

r. de Mézières

St-Sulpice

r. P alatine

r. Garancière

allée du Séminaire

Théatre
National de
l'Odéon

6e

d'Assas

r. H. Chevalier

Casette

Madame

r. Férou

r. Servandoni

Palais du
Luxembourg

de Médicis

Rennes

M

5

r. de Vaugirard

Musée de
Luxembourg

Fontaine
de Médicis

Luxembourg

RER

6

bd. St-Michel

bd. Raspail

r. de Fleurus

Guynemer

Jardin du
Luxembourg

Alliance
Française

r. Huysmans

Madame

Musée de
Minéralogie

Notre-Dame
des Champs

M

d'Assas

École
National
Supérieure
des Mines

Luxembourg

RER

Notre-Dame des Champs

place et Square
Ozanam

r. Auguste Comte

r. du Montparnasse

r. Stanislas

bd. Raspail

r. Vavin

| 0 | | 1/4 Mi |
| 0 | .25 Km | |

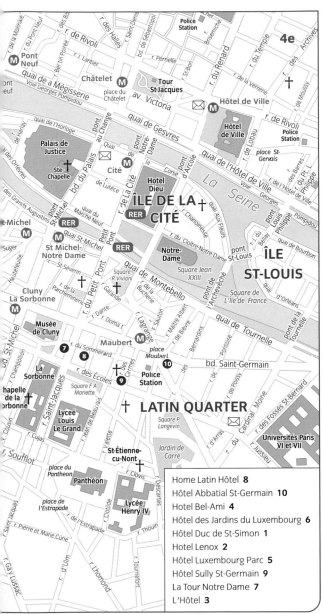

Home Latin Hôtel **8**
Hôtel Abbatial St-Germain **10**
Hotel Bel-Ami **4**
Hôtel des Jardins du Luxembourg **6**
Hôtel Duc de St-Simon **1**
Hotel Lenox **2**
Hôtel Luxembourg Parc **5**
Hôtel Sully St-Germain **9**
La Tour Notre Dame **7**
L'Hôtel **3**

# Paris Hotels **A to Z**

*Fashonistas flock to the trendy Axial Beaubourg.*

**★★ Axial Beaubourg** MARAIS
This restored hotel is one of the city's trendiest cutting-edge hotels, with a location near the Louvre. Its exposed beams, old stones, and wood floors give it old-world charm with modern convenience. *11 rue du Temple, 4th.* ☎ *01-42-72-72-22. www.axialbeaubourg.com. 39 units. Doubles 155€–200€. AE, DC, MC, V. Métro: Hôtel-de-Ville. Map p 140.*

**★ Concorde St-Lazare** ST LAZARE
One of the neighborhood's best hotels, this 19th-century hostelry has been tastefully upgraded to modern standards. The large guest rooms have high ceilings and big windows. *108 rue St-Lazare, 8th.* ☎ *800/888-4747 in the U.S., or 01-40-08-44-44. www.concordest lazare-paris.com. 256 units. Doubles 360€–450€. AE, DC, MC, V. Métro: St-Lazare. Map p 139.*

**★★★ Four Seasons Hotel George V** GEORGE V   This hotel is one of the best in the world, and

has hosted presidents and royalty. Guest rooms are lavish, large, and luxurious, with equally spacious bathrooms. Prices are unsurprisingly high. *31 av. George-V, 8th.* ☎ *800/ 332-33442 in the U.S., or 01-49-52-70-00. www.fourseasons.com. 245 units. Doubles 670€–890€. AE, DC, MC, V. Métro: George-V. Map p 139.*

**★ Galileo Hôtel** CONCORDE   This delightful town house sits a short stroll away from the Champs-Elysées and is the epitome of French elegance and charm. Rooms are understated, done in cocoa and beige. Bathrooms are good-size, prices moderate. *54 rue Galilée, 8th.* ☎ *01-47-20-66-06. 27 units. Doubles 153€. AE, DC, MC, V. Métro: Charles-de-Gaulle–Etoile or George-V. Map p 139.*

**kids Home Latin Hôtel** ST-GERMAIN-DES-PRES   This is one of Paris's best-known budget hotels, beloved by its acolytes for its proximity to the Luxembourg Gardens, its clean functional rooms, and its friendly staff. It has good-size family rooms as well.

*If price is no object, a stay at the Four Seasons won't disappoint.*

15–17 rue du Sommerard, 5th. ☎ 01-43-26-25-21. www.homelatin hotel.com. 54 units. Doubles 91€. AE, DC, MC, V. Métro: St-Michel or Maubert-Mutualité. Map p 142.

**Hôtel Abbatial St-Germain**
ST-GERMAIN-DES-PRES   The historic building that houses this hotel has been renovated to a modern standard without losing its charm. The small guest rooms are furnished with Louis XVI reproductions. Bathrooms are tiny but have all you should need. 46 bd. St-Germain, 5th. ☎ 01-46-34-02-12. www.abbatial. com. 43 units. Doubles 127€–150€. AE, MC, V. Métro: Cluny–La Sorbonne. Map p 142.

**★★ Hôtel Balzac** GEORGE V
This Belle Epoque mansion is sleekly designed with modern furniture, elegant touches, and king-size beds. Most have good-size bathrooms as well. Staff is effortlessly efficient. 6 rue Balzac, 8th. ☎ 800/457-4000 In the U.S., or 01-44-35-18-00. 70 units. Doubles 380€–460€. AE, DC, MC, V. Métro: George-V. Map p 139.

**★ Hotel Bel-Ami** LATIN QUARTER
Recently restored, floor by floor, this sleek, arts-conscious hotel has a minimalist look with a clean design aesthetic. Earth-toned guest rooms have a Zen-like air, with a minimum of furniture. 7–11 rue St-Benoit, 6th. ☎ 01-49-27-09-33. www.hotel-bel-ami.com. 115 units. Doubles 260€–380€. AE, DC, MC, V. Métro: St-Germain-des-Prés. Map p 142.

**Hôtel Bellevue & Chariot d'Or**
LES HALLES   Don't be fooled by the grand facade—the rooms are simple and, as they say in the business, "cozy," but they're also quiet and comfortable. Staff is very helpful. 39 rue de Turbigo, 3rd. ☎ 01-48-87-45-60. www.hotelbellevue75.com. 59 units. Doubles 60€. AE, DC, MC, V. Métro: Châtelet or Les Halles. Map p 140.

**Hôtel Bonséjour** MONTMARTRE
One of the best deals in Montmartre, this hotel is charmingly equipped with antiques. There's no elevator serving its six floors, and communal toilet rooms are located on the landings. But boy, is it cheap. 11 rue Burq, 18th. ☎ 01-42-54-22-53. 34 units, none with toilet, some with showers. Doubles 32€. No credit cards. Métro: Abbesses. Map p 139.

**★ Hôtel Britannique** LOUVRE
Tastefully modern and plush, this place has cultivated a kind of English graciousness. Guest rooms are small, but nicely appointed and soundproof. 20 av. Victoria, 1st. ☎ 01-42-33-74-59. www.hotel-britannic.com. 39 units. Doubles 170€–180€. AE, DC, MC, V. Métro: Châtelet. Map p 140.

**★ Hôtel Burgundy** MADELEINE
One of the best values in a pricey neighborhood, the Burgundy is composed of two town houses— one a former bordello, one where Baudelaire wrote his poetry. Guest rooms are simple but effortlessly elegant. 8 rue Duphot, 1st. ☎ 01-42-60-34-12. www.burgundyhotel. com. 89 units. Doubles 165€–195€. AE, DC, MC, V. Métro: Madeleine or Concorde. Map p 140.

**★ Hôtel Caron de Beaumar-chais** MARAIS   This attractive old-world hotel has ancient stone floors,

*Hotel Caron de Beaumarchais offers good value for its moderate rates.*

antique reproductions, and gorgeous fabrics. Some rooms have sweeping balcony views. *12 rue Vielle du Temple, 4th.* ☎ *01-42-72-34-12. www.carondebeaumarchais.com. 19 units. Doubles 120€–152€. AE, MC, V. Métro: St-Paul or Hotel-de-Ville. Map p 140.*

★ **Hôtel Chopin** GRANDS BOULE-VARDS  I love this intimate, eccentric hotel, just off the Grands Boulevards. The Victorian lobby has elegant woodwork, rooms are comfortably furnished, and the staff is friendly. *10 bd. Montmartre, 9th.* ☎ *01-47-70-58-10. 36 units. Doubles 73€–97€. Métro: Grands Boulevards. Map p 140.*

★★ **Hôtel Costes** CONCORDE A favorite of the rich and famous for its style and location close to fashionable shopping, this town house–style hotel evokes the Gilded Age, particularly in the guest rooms. Many are small, but all are ornate and well equipped. *239 rue St-Honoré, 1st.* ☎ *01-42-44-50-50. 82 units. Doubles 400€–700€. AE, DC, MC, V. Métro: Tuileries or Concorde. Map p 140.*

★★★ **Hôtel de Crillon** CONCORDE This hotel, which sits across the street from the U.S. Embassy, provides a convenient and elegant home away from home for American CEOs and diplomats. It's housed in a 200-year-old former palace rich with tapestries, gilt, brocade, chandeliers, antiques, and art. Fit for a king. *10 place de la Concorde, 8th.* ☎ *800/223-6800 in the U.S., or 01-44-71-15-00. www.crillon.com. 147 units. Doubles 575€–655€. AE, DC, MC, V. Métro: Concorde. Map p 139.*

**Hôtel de la Place de Vosges** MARAIS  This charming, well-managed little hotel was built some 350 years ago, at the same time as the lovely square for which it's named. The cozy rooms have beamed ceilings. *12 rue de Birague,* *4th.* ☎ *01-42-72-60-46. 16 units. Doubles 120€–140€. AE, MC, V. Métro: Bastille. Map p 140.*

★★ **Hôtel de Lutèce** ILE ST LOUIS The tastefully furnished and relaxing rooms at this grand country house–style hotel occasionally lure low-key celebrities and lesser royalty. Fireplaces, antiques, and paintings create a refined atmosphere. *65 rue St-Louis-en-l'Ile.* ☎ *01-43-26-23-52. www.hotel-ile-saintlouis.com. 23 units. Doubles 158€. AE, MC, V. Métro: Pont Marie or Cité. Map p 140.*

★ **Hôtel des Jardins du Luxembourg** ST-GERMAIN-DES-PRES This grand Victorian building of honey-colored stone with ornate iron balconies overlooks a quiet street. Guest rooms have high ceilings, and some have Provençal tiles, ornate moldings, and Art Deco furniture. *5 impasse Royer-Collard, 5th.* ☎ *01-40-46-08-88. 25 units. Doubles 139€–149€. AE, DC, MC, V. Métro: Cluny–La Sorbonne. Map p 142.*

*Shoppers will appreciate Hôtel Costes's proximity to fine boutiques.*

*A junior suite at the Hôtel du Louvre.*

Paris Hotels **A to Z**

147

### ★ Hôtel du Bourg Tibourg

MARAIS   Hotels with far less style can cost twice as much as this well-located place. Rooms are small but comfortable, with romantic, modern decor and lush fabrics in everything from leopard print to stripes. *19 rue du Bourg-Tibourg, 4th.* ☎ *01-42-78-47-39. www. hoteldubourgtibourg.com. 30 units. Doubles 200€–250€. AE, MC, V. Métro: Hôtel-de-Ville. Map p 140.*

### ★ Hôtel Duc de St-Simon

INVALIDES   A sweet courtyard offers your first glimpse of this hopelessly romantic hotel that seduced the likes of Lauren Bacall. Rooms are filled with antiques, objets d'art, and lush fabrics. Some have terraces over-looking a garden. *14 rue de St-Simon, 7th.* ☎ *01-44-39-20-20. 34 units. Doubles 220€–250€. AE, MC, V. Métro: Rue du Bac. Map p 142.*

### ★★ Hôtel du Louvre LOUVRE

This former home of painter Camille Pissarro is now a sort of Belle Epoque palace hotel, resplendent with mar-ble, bronze, and gilt galore. Guest rooms are stuffed with antiques and heavy fabrics. *Place André Malraux, 1st.* ☎ *800/888-4747 in the U.S. & Canada, or 01-44-58-38-38. www. hoteldulouvre.com. 177 units. Doubles 455€–500€. AE, DC, MC, V. Métro: Palais Royal or Louvre Rivoli. Map p 140.*

**Hôtel du 7th Art** MARAIS   This 17th-century building is actually a his-toric monument, but don't expect great luxury. Rooms are tiny, with white walls and exposed beams, each with an even smaller bathroom. The art consists of movie stills and other film-related subjects. The five-story building has no elevator. *20 rue St-Paul, 4th.* ☎ *01-44-54-85-00. 23 units. Doubles 75€–130€. AE, DC, MC, V. Métro: St-Paul. Map p 140.*

### ★ Hôtel Elysées Ceramic

CONCORDE   An ornate ceramic facade helps make this celebrated Art Nouveau building easy to find. The clean, modern, attractive rooms are less over-the-top. *34 av. de Wagram, 8th.* ☎ *01-42-27-20-30. www.elysees-ceramic.com. 57 units. Doubles 200€. AE, DC, MC, V. Métro: Charles-de-Gaulle–Etoile. Map p 139.*

**Hôtel Ermitage** MONTMARTRE Built in 1870, this sweet hotel looks like a small villa. A brief stroll from the Sacré Coeur in romantic, hilly Montmartre, it offers sweeping views of Paris. Rooms have exposed beams and flowered wallpaper. *24 rue Lamarck, 18th.* ☎ *01-42-64-79-22. 12 units. Doubles 86€ w/breakfast. No credit cards. Métro: Lamarck-Caulaincourt. Map p 139.*

### ★ Hôtel Langlois GRANDS

BOULEVARDS   This charming hotel in a restored town house has extra touches like a curving Parisian stair-well and an antique, wrought-iron elevator. Rooms are smallish but generally tasteful, some with fireplaces. *63 rue St-Lazare, 9th.* ☎ *01-48-74-78-24. www.hotel-langlois.com. 27 units. Doubles 96€–110€. AE, DC, MC, V. Métro: Trinité. Map p 140.*

*Hôtel Langlois boasts interesting architectural details and moderate rates.*

★ **Hotel Lenox** INVALIDES  The staff will happily fill you in on the literary history of the hotel. (T. S. Eliot convinced James Joyce to stay here after Ezra Pound fell in love with the place.) The bar alone is worth a visit. The modern guest rooms, reached via a glass elevator, are decorated in creamy tones with rich blue accents and some antique reproductions. Some rooms have wondrous views. *9 rue de l'Université, 7th.* ☎ *01-42-96-10-95. www.lenoxsaintgermain. com. 40 units. Doubles 120€–205€. AE, DC, MC, V. Métro: St-Germain-des-Prés. Map p 142.*

★★ **Hôtel Luxembourg Parc** LATIN QUARTER  As the name implies, this hotel is near the Luxembourg Gardens, a lovely place for summer strolls. Everything at this 17th-century palace is designed with elegance in mind, from the guest rooms with Louis XV furniture to the bar. *42 rue de Vaugirad, 6th.* ☎ *01-53-10-36-50. www.luxembourg-paris-hotel.com. 23 units. Doubles 200€–475€. AE, DC, MC, V. Métro: Luxembourg. Map p 142.*

★★ **Hôtel Meurice** CONCORDE Salvador Dalí once made this hotel his headquarters. It's gorgeous, with perfectly preserved mosaic floors, hand-carved moldings, and an Art Nouveau glass roof. Rooms are sumptuous and individually decorated, some with fluffy clouds and blue skies painted on the ceilings. *228 rue de Rivoli, 1st.* ☎ *01-44-58-10-10. www.meuricehotel.com. 160 units. Doubles 650€–760€. AE, DC, MC, V. Métro: Tuileries or Concorde. Map p 140.*

★★★ **Hôtel Ritz** CONCORDE This is Europe's greatest hotel, and an enduring symbol of elegance. The public rooms are furnished with museum-quality antiques, and each guest room is filled with reproductions, fine rugs, marble fireplaces, tapestries, brass beds, and cords to summon maids. Ah, the luxury. *15 place Vendôme, 1st.* ☎ *800/223-6800 in North America, or 01-43-16-30-30. www.ritzparis.com. 175 units. Doubles 610€–770€. AE, DC, MC, V. Métro: Opéra or Concorde. Map p 140.*

★★ **Hôtel Royal St-Honoré** CONCORDE  Recently remodeled, this oasis of charm attracts hip guests drawn by nearby shops like Chanel and Hermès. Contemporary styling contrasts nicely with antique furnishings. The bar is *très chic*. *221 rue St-Honoré, 1st.* ☎ *01-42-60-32-79. www.hotel-royal-st-honore.com. 72 units. Doubles 200€–400€ w/breakfast. AE, DC, MC, V. Métro: Tuileries. Map p 140.*

★ **Hôtel Saintonge** MARAIS Rooms are small, but the exposed beams, old masonry, and narrow hallways climbing seven stories create a cozy atmosphere. Breakfast is served in the old cellar. *16 rue Saintonge, 3rd.* ☎ *01-42-77-91-13. www.hotel marais.com. 23 units Doubles 115€. AE, DC, MC, V. Métro: Filles du Calvaire or République. Map p 140.*

★ **Hôtel St-Louis** ILE ST LOUIS A charming family atmosphere reigns at this antique-filled hotel in a 17th-century town house. Rooms are small but well decorated, there are lots of lovely touches, and the location is excellent. Great value for the price. *75 rue St-Louis-en-l'Ile, 4th.* ☎ *01-46-34-04-80. www.hotelsaint louis.com. 19 units. Doubles 140€– 220€. MC, V. Métro: Pont Marie or St-Michel-Notre-Dame. Map p 140.*

★ **Hôtel Sully St-Germain** ST-GERMAIN-DES-PRES With its medieval-style decor and exquisite antiques, this is a good option for the money. Stylish guest rooms have brass beds and stone walls. *31 rue des Ecoles, 5th.* ☎ *01-43-26-56-02. www.hotel-paris-sully.com. 61 units. Doubles 160€–200€. AE, DC, MC, V. Métro: Maubert Mutualité. Map p 142.*

★ **Hôtel Victoires Opéra** LES HALLES This sleek little charmer offers reasonably priced lodging at the edge of the Marais. The place looks fabulous, with stark white walls balanced with taupe trim and black touches. Rooms are simply but elegantly decorated in colonial style, some with polished wood floors, but are a bit small. Skip the hotel breakfast and go out for fabulous pastries from Stohrer across the street instead *56 rue Montorgueil, 2nd.* ☎ *01-42-36-41-08. www.hotelvictoiresopera.com. 24 units. Doubles 213€–274€. AE, DC, MC, V. Métro: Les Halles. Map p 140.*

★ **La Tour Notre Dame** ST-GERMAIN-DES-PRES This well-located hotel (opposite the Sorbonne) has been intelligently renovated. Guest rooms have exposed beams and a romantic feel, with Liberty prints and Empire furniture. *20 rue du Sommerard, 5th.* ☎ *01-43-54-47-60. www.tour-notre-dame.com. 48 units. Doubles 129€– 169€. AE, DC, MC, V. Métro: Cluny– La Sorbonne. Map p 142.*

*A suite at the Hôtel Luxembourg Parc.*

**Le Petit Châtelet** HOTEL DE VILLE This small hotel is popular with musicians from nearby jazz clubs. Its warm decor is colorful and pleasant, often with a music theme. Rooms are small and a bit battered, but the hotel is a good choice for those on a budget. It has six floors and no elevator. *9 rue St-Denis, 1st.* ☎ *01-42-33-32-31. 15 units. Doubles 70€. AE, MC, V. Métro: Châtelet or Hôtel-de-Ville. Map p 140.*

★ **L'Hôtel** LATIN QUARTER The hotel where Oscar Wilde died is now one of the Left Bank's most distinctive boutique hotels. Each guest room is different, some with fireplaces, some with fabric-covered walls. There's a swimming pool in the cellar. *13 rue des Beaux-Arts, 6th.* ☎ *01-44-41-99-00. www.l-hotel. com. 20 units. Doubles 280€–640€. AE, DC, MC, V. Métro: St-Germain-des-Prés. Map p 142.*

★★★ **Park Hyatt Vendôme** OPERA This hotel is a citadel of luxurious 21st-century living. High ceilings and colonnades make the hotel airy and dramatic. The sleek, modern fittings add to the luxury, as do the modern art and rich fabrics. *3–5 rue de la Paix, 2nd.* ☎ *01-48-71-12-24. www.paris.vendome.hyatt.com. 177 units. Doubles 410€–600€. AE, DC, MC, V. Métro: Tuileries or Opéra. Map p 140.*

★ **Pavillon de Paris** PIGALLE This gem of a hotel makes up in style for what it lacks in size. It's sleekly decorated with a minimalist aesthetic featuring dark wood and modern art. There's a cool bar, too. *7 rue de Parme, 9th.* ☎ *01-55-31-60-00. www.pavillondeparis.com. 30 units. Doubles 255€–296€. AE, DC, MC, V. Métro: Liège or Place de Clichy. Map p 139.*

★★★ **Plaza Athénée** CONCORDE This Art Nouveau marvel has been a favorite of celebrities for so long that it can count Mata Hari among its guests. It's superbly decorated, with marble floors, gorgeous glass-and-iron doors, and rich fabrics. *25 av. Montaigne, 8th.* ☎ *866/732-1106 in the U.S., or 01-53-67-66-65. www.plaza-athenee-paris.com. 188 units. Doubles 690€–750€. AE, DC, MC, V. Métro: Franklin-D.-Roosevelt or Alma Marceau. Map p 139.*

★★ **Terrass Hôtel** MONTMARTRE This hotel is a find, with a marble-floored lobby, blond-oak paneling, antiques, and paintings. Guest rooms have high ceilings and sophisticated decor. *12 rue Joseph de Maistre, 18th.* ☎ *01-46-06-72-85. www.terrass-hotel.com. 100 units. Doubles 248€–290€ w/breakfast. Métro: Place de Clichy or Blanche. Map p 139.*

kids **Timhôtel Le Louvre** LOUVRE The Timhôtels, part of a new breed of moderately priced family-friendly hotels cropping up in France, tend to be modern, with a monochromatic color scheme. Smallish rooms, but a great location. *4 rue Croix des Petits-Champs, 1st.* ☎ *01-42-60-34-86. www.timhotel.fr. 56 units. 125€–150€. Children under 12 stay for free. AE, DC, MC, V. Métro: Palais Royal. Map p 140.* ●

*Hôtel Meurice's "winter garden," with Art Nouveau glass roof.*

# Decadent Versailles

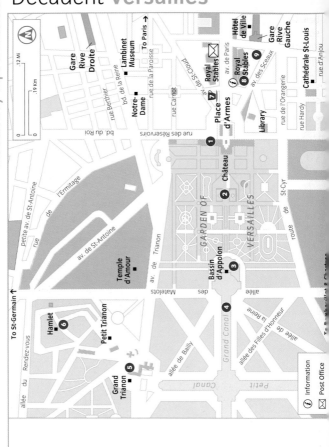

ⓘ Information
☒ Post Office

**Y**es, it's touristy, and yes, it will be crowded in the summer, but come anyway. This extraordinary palace must be seen to be believed, and it is well worth the 35-minute journey to the Parisian suburbs. It took 40,000 workers 50 years to convert Louis XIII's hunting lodge into this extravagant palace. Work started in 1661, and before it was finished, entire forests had been moved to make way for its extensive gardens. It was here that French royalty lived a life so decadent in a time of widespread poverty that their excesses spurred a revolution.

*This bronze statue sits on the edge of a lake in the Versailles gardens.*

largest is the Hercules Salon, where the ceiling is painted with the *Apotheosis of Hercules*. The elaborate Mercury Salon is where the body of Louis XIV lay in state after his death. But the apartments pale in comparison to the 71m long (233-ft.) Hall of Mirrors. No superlative is super enough to describe the hall's size—not to mention its walls, ceilings, or chandeliers. The Hall of Mirrors was designed to reflect sunlight back into the garden and remind people that the "Sun King" lived here. In 1919, the treaty ending World War I was signed in this hall. Elsewhere in the palace there's an impressive library with delicately

*A bedroom in the Palace of Versailles.*

**❶ ★★★ Palace of Versailles.** One of the first things you'll notice when you arrive is that the vast palace is actually dwarfed by the grounds, which stretch for miles. Inside the palace, it's all over the top, all the time. Not a corner was left unpainted. Every lily? Gilded. The king and his family lived in the Petits Appartements much of the time, where the king's apartment and the queen's bedchamber are exquisitely overdone. The six Grands Appartements are grand indeed, and these were just for the king's sycophants and their staffs. The

*Some 200km (120 miles) of channels, trenches, and aqueducts feed the fountains at Versailles.*

carved panels, designed by the architect Jacques-Ange Gabriel, and a Clock Room with a gilded bronze astronomical clock. It was made in 1753 and is supposed to keep perfect time until 9999. Gabriel also designed the Opéra in 1748, where Louis XVI and Marie Antoinette's wedding banquet was held in 1770. ⏱ *2 hr.*

**②** ★★★ **Gardens of Versailles.** These vast, varied, vainglorious gardens were created by the landscape artist Le Nôtre, who used lakes, canals, geometric flower beds, long avenues, fountains, and statuary to create a French Eden. Over recent decades, a painstaking effort to replant and restore the gardens has had excellent results, and the grounds are breathtaking (not just from the exertion required to traverse them). ⏱ *2 hr.*

**③** **Apollo Fountain.** At one time, 1,400 fountains splashed and burbled around the grounds. The most famous surviving fountain depicts Apollo's chariot being pulled from the water by four horses surrounded by Tritons. As with many of the fountains, much has been lost to the ages, but much is being restored as well.

**④** **Grand Canal.** The 1.6km (1-mile) canal is surrounded by lush planted forests crossed by straight paths. So precise was Le Nôtre's design that on St. Louis Day (Aug 25) the sun sets in perfect alignment with the Grand Canal. Louis kept a fleet of gondolas for parties on the water. Today you can rent a boat and paddle about, but it's a bit anticlimactic without the sails, ladies in gowns, and minstrels. Oh, well. You can also rent a bike to cycle through the gardens, and there's even a miniature train.

**⑤** ★★ **Grand Trianon & Petit Trianon.** Many believe the Italianate palace known as the Grand Trianon is more interesting than the main palace. Made of pink marble, it was designed in 1687 to house staff, and was later the home of Napoleon and his family. The gardens here differ greatly from those connected with the main palace, which is not surprising since they were designed by Jacques-Ange Gabriel. He also designed the Petit Trianon nearby, which was where Louis XV held "meetings" with Madame de Pompadour. Later, it was Marie Antoinette's favorite part of the Versailles grounds. ⏱ *30 min. Can be reached by the "Petit Train" from the Parterre Nord, fare 5€. Admission 5€. Apr–Oct daily noon–6:30pm; Nov–Mar daily noon–5:30pm.*

**⑥** **Hameau de la Reine.** The lovely, thatch-roofed house beyond the Petit Trianon is a fanciful faux farmhouse built for Marie Antoinette, who liked to play shepherdess.

*This picturesque faux farming village was built for Marie Antoinette in 1783.*

**7 Le Quai No. 1.** Stop for a bite to eat at this informal bistro with a view of the palace. Imaginative seafood dishes like stuffed baby mullet with sweet-basil sauce are your best bet. The prix fixe menu is a real bargain. *1 av. de St-Cloud.* ☎ *01-39-50-42-26. $$*

**8 Grande Ecurie.** The famous Versailles horses are kept in high style here, and trained in a variety of equine performance arts. You can watch the horse trainers at work, or take in a performance on weekends. ⏱ *30 min. Near the palace entrance on av. Rockefeller.* ☎ *01-39-02-07-14. Admission 7€. Performances 15€. Tues–Fri 9am–1pm; Sat–Sun 11am–2pm. Performances Sat–Sun 2:15–3pm.*

**9 Musée des Carosses.** This tiny museum holds the royal coaches used for special occasions like baptisms, weddings, funerals, and coronations, as well as adorable royal sleighs, which skidded down the Grand Canal in the winter. ⏱ *30 min. Next to the Grande Ecurie.* ☎ *01-30-83-77-88. Admission 1.90€. Mar–Apr Sat–Sun 2–5:30pm; May–Sept Sat–Sun 2–6:30pm.*

## Versailles: Practical Matters

Versailles (www.chateauversailles.fr) is open May through September, Tuesday through Sunday from 9am to 6:30pm; October through April, Tuesday through Sunday from 9am to 5:30pm. Admission is 7.50€. Credit cards are not accepted. There's a discount after 3:30pm, and free admission the first Sunday of the month from October to March. Admission to the gardens is free; they are open 7am to dusk in summer, 8am to dusk in winter. You can purchase an audioguide (in English) for 4€. (Go to entrance C.) Guided tours (in English or French) also cost 4€. (Go to entrance D.) You can take a horse-drawn carriage ride around the park for 7€ and up. Get tickets for Versailles in advance by calling ☎ 01-30-83-77-77, or ask at your hotel—some will arrange tickets for guests.

To get here, take a train from Gare Montparnasse or Gare St-Lazare to Versailles–Rive Droite. You can also take bus no.171 from Paris's pont de Sèvres to Versailles's place d'Armes. By car, take the D10 or the A13 from Paris to the Versailles–Château exit. The trip to Versailles takes about 30 to 40 minutes by car or train.

# Disneyland Paris

1. Main Street, USA
2. Frontierland
3. Adventureland
4. Fantasyland
5. Auberge de Cendrillon
6. Discoveryland
7. Village Disney

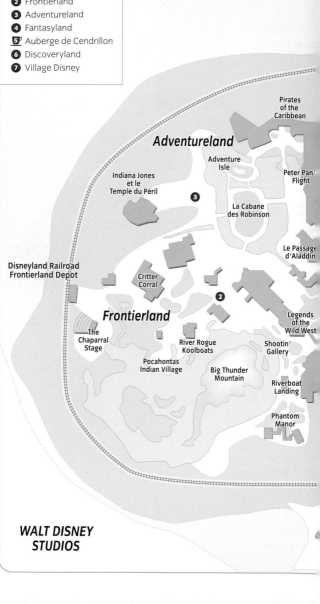

Pirates of the Caribbean

**Adventureland**

Adventure Isle

Peter Pan' Flight

Indiana Jones et le Temple du Péril

3

La Cabane des Robinson

Le Passage d'Aladdin

Disneyland Railroad Frontierland Depot

Critter Corral

2

**Frontierland**

Legends of the Wild West

The Chaparral Stage

River Rogue Koolboats

Shootin' Gallery

Pocahontas Indian Village

Big Thunder Mountain

Riverboat Landing

Phantom Manor

*WALT DISNEY STUDIOS*

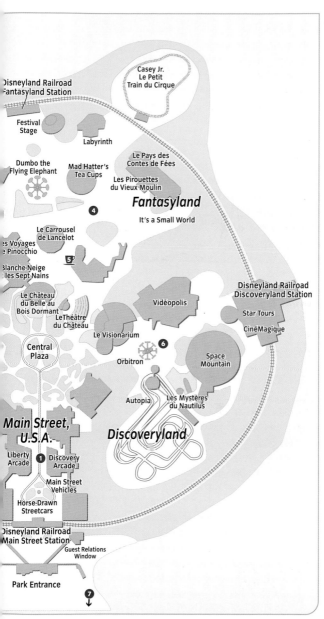

Disneyland Railroad Fantasyland Station

Casey Jr. Le Petit Train du Cirque

Festival Stage

Labyrinth

Dumbo the Flying Elephant

Mad Hatter's Tea Cups

Le Pays des Contes de Fées

Les Pirouettes du Vieux Moulin

*Fantasyland*

It's a Small World

❹

Le Carrousel de Lancelot

es Voyages e Pinocchio

❺

Blanche-Neige les Sept Nains

Le Château du Belle au Bois Dormant

LeThéâtre du Château

Le Visionarium

Disneyland Railroad Discoveryland Station

Vidéopolis

Star Tours

CinéMagique

❻

Central Plaza

Orbitron

Space Mountain

Autopia

Les Mystères du Nautilus

*Main Street, U.S.A.*

*Discoveryland*

Liberty Arcade

❶ Discovery Arcade

Main Street Vehicles

Horse-Drawn Streetcars

Disneyland Railroad Main Street Station

Guest Relations Window

Park Entrance

❼
↓

With 50 million annual visitors, Disneyland Paris has triumphed over early Euro-snobbery, and is the number-one tourist attraction in France. It's also a blessing for travelers with kids who have wearied of the museums and churches and just want to go on the rides for 1 day, pleasepleaseplease! Overall, there's little difference between this amusement park and those in Florida and California, except here the 9€ cheeseburger comes with *pommes frites* instead of fries.

**1 Main Street, USA.** Immediately after entering the park, you'll find yourself in an idealized American town, complete with horse-drawn carriages and street-corner barbershop quartets. If you're here after dark, you can take in the surprisingly lovely Electric Parade (nightly July–Aug), when all the Disney characters pass by along with brightly illuminated floats.

**2 Frontierland.** In this "pretend America" it's a conveniently short hop to the West, particularly if you board one of the steam-powered trains that takes you through a Grand Canyon diorama to Frontierland. A tribe of French actors offers up rootin' tootin' entertainment at Pocahontas's Indian village. In summer, if it gets too hot, you and the kids can ride a paddle-wheel steamship.

**3 Adventureland.** The trains will take you on to Adventureland, where swashbuckling pirates battle near the Swiss Family Robinson's treehouse. If that's too tame, head for the Indiana Jones and the Temple of Peril. It travels backwards at breakneck speed, the only Disneyland roller coaster in the world to do so.

**4 Fantasyland.** Young children will be charmed by Sleeping Beauty's Castle (Le Château de la Belle au Bois Dormant) and its idealized interpretation of a French château, complete with the obligatory fire-breathing dragon in its dungeon. From here, a visit with Dumbo the Flying Elephant may be necessary, and perhaps a whirl on the giant teacup ride. The (unintentionally) kitsch It's a Small World is home to dolls in national costumes, and unfortunately reinforces mindless stereotypes.

*One of the park's steam trains.*

*Sleeping Beauty's castle.*

**5 Auberge de Cendrillon.** If you're looking for a nice sit-down lunch, try this restaurant for traditional French dining in Cinderella's country inn. (Reservations are recommended.) Otherwise, take your pick from any of the dozens of dining options scattered throughout the park—standards are pretty high here, so you should feel comfortable going with whatever looks good. *Fantasyland.* ☎ 01-64-74-24-02. $$$

**6 Discoveryland.** Explore the visions of the future displayed here, with designs drawn from the works of Leonardo da Vinci, Jules Verne, and H. G. Wells, as well as from more modern fictional creations like *Star Wars.* This is the park's most popular area, and includes its own version of Space Mountain, which emulates Jules Verne's version of what a trip from Earth to the moon would be like.

**7 Village Disney.** This haven for adults features an indoor/outdoor layout that's a cross between a California shopping mall and Coney Island boardwalk. On either side of the central walkways are endless options—dance clubs, snack bars, restaurants, shops, and bars. (Disney bars? It's just too weird.)

## Disneyland Paris: Practical Matters

Disneyland Paris (☎ 01-60-30-60-53; www.disneylandparis.com) is located in the suburb of Marne-la-Vallée, about 32km (20 miles) east of Paris. To get here, take the RER Line A to the Marney-la-Vallée/Chessy stop (about 40 min.), which is within walking distance of the park. By car, take A-4 east from Paris to exit 14. Parking is 8€ per day. Admission for 1 day is 40€ adults, 30€ children ages 3 to 12, free for kids under 3. The park is open daily from 9am to 8pm in July and August; daily 9am to 6pm September through June.

The resort was designed as a total vacation destination, so within the enormous compound there's not only the park with its five "lands," but also six hotels, campgrounds, Village Disney entertainment center, a 27-hole golf course, and dozens of restaurants and shops.

# The Cathedral at Chartres

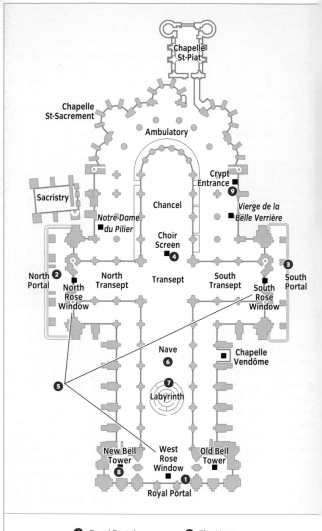

Chapelle St-Piat

Chapelle St-Sacrement

Ambulatory

Sacristy

Crypt Entrance ❾

Chancel

Notre-Dame du Pilier

Vierge de la Belle Verrière

Choir Screen ❹

North Portal ❷

North Rose Window

North Transept

Transept

South Transept

South Rose Window

South Portal ❸

Nave ❻

Chapelle Vendôme

❺

❼ Labyrinth

New Bell Tower ❽

West Rose Window

Old Bell Tower

❶ Royal Portal

❶ Royal Portal
❷ North Portal
❸ South Portal
❹ Choir Screen
❺ Rose Windows

❻ The Nave
❼ Floor Labyrinth
❽ New Bell Tower
❾ Crypts

At the opposite end of the spiritual spectrum from decadent Versailles, Chartres represented the highest architectural and theological aspirations of the Middle Ages in France. The cathedral was much the same in medieval times as it is now, which should give you a sense of how impressive it must have been in 1260, when it was completed. Rodin described it as the French Acropolis, and once you've seen it you'll be hard pressed to disagree with him.

*The Royal Portal.*

**❶ Royal Portal.** From the first moment I saw the Royal Portal, I was seduced. (Probably not the right word to use when talking about a church, but still . . . ) The sculpted bodies around it are elongated and garbed in long, flowing robes, but their faces are almost disturbingly lifelike—frowning, winking, and smiling. Christ is shown at the Second Coming—his descent to Earth on the right, his ascent back to Heaven on the left.

**❷ North Portal.** Both the North Portal and the South Portal (see next stop) are carved with biblical images, including the expulsion of Adam and Eve from the Garden of Eden.

**❸ South Portal.** This doorway is carved with the images of saints. The martyrs are carved in painful detail on the right door. Apostles get the center, and confessors the left door.

**❹ Choir Screen.** This celebrated screen dates to the 16th century. It has 40 niches holding statues of biblical figures. Don't be so dazzled by all the stained glass (see next stop) that you overlook its intricate carvings.

**❺ ★★★ Rose Windows.** No cathedral in the world can match Chartres for its 12th-century glass (saved from damage during World War I and World War II by parishioners who removed it piece by piece and stored the pieces safely). It gave the world a new color— Chartres blue—and it is absolutely exceptional. All of its windows are glorious, but the three rose windows may be the best.

*One of the cathedral's magnificent rose windows.*

*The choir screen.*

**6 The Nave.** At about 17m (54 ft.), the nave at Chartres is the widest in France, and its soaring ceilings are as impressive as ever. The wooden *Notre-Dame du Piller (Virgin of the Pillar)* to the left of the choir dates from the 14th century. In the center of the nave is the mysterious labyrinth. (See below.)

**7 Floor Labyrinth.** Many Gothic cathedrals once had labyrinths like the one on the floor of the nave, but virtually all were destroyed over time, so this one is very rare (not that this stops the church from occasionally covering it with chairs). The meaning of labyrinths has been lost to time; one theory claims they represent the passage of the soul to heaven.

**8 New Bell Tower.** The enthusiastic, those not afraid of heights, and the physically fit may want to climb to the top of this tower, from the peak of which you can see for miles. *Admission 4€. Closed noon–2pm.*

**9 Crypts.** Those who prefer underground crypts to the dizzying heights of the tower will find that they can only visit the one here as part of a French-language tour. *Admission 1.65€. Times vary depending on demand.* ●

## Chartres: Practical Matters

From Paris's Gare Montparnasse, trains run direct to Chartres (1 hr.). By car, take A-10/A-11 southwest from the Périphérique and follow signs to Le Mans and Chartres (about 1½ hr.). The cathedral is open May through October daily from 8am to 8pm, and November through April daily from 8am to 7:15pm. Admission is free. Guided tours in English are available May through October, Monday through Saturday at noon and 12:45pm; meet at the gift shop. Call ☎ 02-37-21-59-08 for more information.

Any trip to the cathedral should include a visit to the cobbled, medieval streets of Chartres's **Vieux Quartier (Old Quarter),** which stretches from the cathedral down to the Eure River. My favorite street is **rue Chantault,** where the 800-year-old houses have wonderfully colorful facades. Also, stop in at the **Musée des Beaux Arts de Chartres,** right next to the cathedral, at 29 Cloître Notre-Dame (☎ 02-37-36-41-39; admission 2.50€). It has an excellent collection covering the 16th through the 20th centuries. For lunch, try **Le Buisson Ardent,** 10 rue au Lait (☎ 02-37-34-04-66), a traditional French restaurant. The prix-fixe lunches are an excellent value.

# The
# **Savvy Traveler**

# **Before** You Go

## Government Tourist Offices

**IN THE U.S.:** 444 Madison Ave., 16th Floor, New York, NY 10022 (☎ 212/838-7800); 676 N. Michigan Ave., Suite 3214, Chicago, IL 60611 (☎ 312/751-7800); 9454 Wilshire Blvd., Suite 715, Beverly Hills, CA 90212 (☎ 310/271-6665). **IN CANADA:** Maison de la France, 1981 av. McGill College, Suite 490, Montreal, H3A 2W9 (☎ 514/876-9881). **IN THE U.K.:** Maison de la France, 178 Piccadilly, London W1J 9AL (☎ 020/7943-6594). **IN IRELAND:** 10 Suffolk St., IRL-2, Dublin (☎ 01-679-0813). **IN AUSTRALIA:** French Tourist Bureau, 25 Bligh St., Sydney, NSW 2000 (☎ 02/9231-5244).

## The Best Times to Go

Paris gets less crowded in **August,** when the locals traditionally take their annual holiday. However, the cheaper hotels tend to fill up with students and budget travelers, and many of the smaller shops, restaurants, and galleries may be closed. You may want to avoid **late September/early October,** when the annual auto show attracts thousands of enthusiasts.

## Festivals & Special Events

**SPRING.** Part country fair, part mammoth amusement park, the **Foire du Trône** has been going on for over a thousand years. It's held in March. ☎ 01-46-27-52-29. Gather at the Palace of Versailles in April for the musical events of **Les Grandes Eaux Musicales,** when you can promenade through the grounds at their most spectacular. ☎ 01-30-83-78-00. In late May or early June, catch the **French Open Tennis Championships.** ☎ 01-49-10-20-30; www.fft.fr/rolandgarros/fr.

**SUMMER.** During the citywide **Fête de la Musique,** street parties and concerts celebrate the summer solstice (June 21). It's the only day that noise laws don't apply. ☎ 01-40-03-94-70; www.fetedelamusique. culture.fr. See the latest in Gallic aviation technology at the **Paris Air Shows,** held in mid-June. ☎ 01-53-12-33-33; www.salon-du-bourget.fr. The **Tour de France,** Europe's biggest bicycle race, winds across the country throughout July. The finish line is on the Champs-Elysées. ☎ 01-41-33-15-00; www. letour.fr. On **Bastille Day** (July 14), citywide celebrations mark the French Revolution.

**FALL.** The **Biennale des Antiquaires,** held on even-numbered years in mid- to late September, attracts enthusiasts from all over the world for gilded exhibitions of furnishings and objets d'art. www. biennaledesantiquaires.com. Much glitz and glamour surround the **Paris Auto Show,** a showcase for European car design. It's held from late September to early October. ☎ 01-56-88-22-40; www.mondial-automobile.com. The **Prix de l'Arc de Triomphe,** held in October at Hippodrome de Longchamp, is the country's most prestigious horse race. ☎ 01-49-10-20-30; www. france-galop.com. Parisians eagerly await the yearly **release of the Beaujolais Nouveau,** a fruity wine from Burgundy, on the third Thursday in November. Look for signs in cafes, bars, and bistros. During the **Fête d'Art Sacré (Festival of Sacred Art)** in November, a series of classical concerts is held in the five oldest churches in Paris. ☎ 01-44-70-64-10.

**WINTER.** **Fête de St-Sylvestre (New Year's Eve)** is celebrated most boisterously in the Latin Quarter. At midnight the city explodes: Strangers kiss, and the Champs-Elysées and boulevard St-Michel become virtual pedestrian malls. January brings the **International Ready-to-Wear Shows,** where hundreds of designers unveil their visions of what you'll be wearing in 6 months. ☎ *01-44-94-70-00; www.pretparis.com.* In February, **special exhibitions and concerts** designed to brighten up Paris's grayest month pop up all over town. Consult local listings in magazines and papers to find out what's on.

### The Weather

Summers are warm and pleasant, with only a few oppressively hot days. However, air-conditioned hotels are rare, so those few days can be truly miserable. Rain is common throughout the year, especially in winter.

### Useful Websites

- www.paris-touristoffice.com: Comprehensive information about traveling to Paris, including hotels, sightseeing, and notices of special events.

- www.mappy.fr: Online maps and journey planner. Covers Paris and the whole of France.

- www.pagesjaunes.fr: Online phone directory for businesses and services.

- www.culture.fr: Extensive listings of upcoming cultural events.

- www.parissi.com: Guide to the Parisian music scene, with an emphasis on nightclubs.

### Cellphones (Mobile Phones)

If your phone has GSM (Global System for Mobiles) capability, and you have a world-compatible phone, you should be able to make and receive calls from France. Only certain phones have this capability, though, and you should check with your service operator first. Call charges can be high. Alternatively, you can rent a phone through **Cellhire** (www.cellhire.com, www.cellhire.co.uk, and www.cellhire.com.au). After a simple online registration, they will ship a phone (usually with a U.K. number) to your home or office. Usage charges can be astronomical, so read the fine print.

U.K. mobiles work in France; call your service provider before departing your home country to ensure that the international call bar has been switched off and to check call charges, which can be extremely high. Also remember that you are charged for calls you *receive* on a U.K. mobile used abroad.

### Car Rentals

There's very little need to rent a car in Paris, but if you're determined to do so, it's usually cheapest to book

---

**PARIS'S AVERAGE DAILY TEMPERATURE & RAINFALL**

|  | JAN | FEB | MAR | APR | MAY | JUNE |
|---|---|---|---|---|---|---|
| Temp (°F) | 38 | 39 | 46 | 51 | 58 | 64 |
| Temp (°C) | 3 | 4 | 8 | 11 | 14 | 18 |
| Rainfall (in.) | 3.2 | 2.9 | 2.4 | 2.7 | 3.2 | 3.5 |

|  | JULY | AUG | SEPT | OCT | NOV | DEC |
|---|---|---|---|---|---|---|
| Temp (°F) | 66 | 66 | 61 | 53 | 45 | 40 |
| Temp (°C) | 19 | 19 | 16 | 12 | 7 | 4 |
| Rainfall (in.) | 3.3 | 3.7 | 3.3 | 3.0 | 3.5 | 3.1 |

a car online before you leave your home country. Try **Hertz** (www.hertz.com), **Avis** (www.avis.com), or **Budget** (www.budget.com). You should also consider **AutoEurope** (www.autoeurope.com), which sends you a pre-paid voucher, locking in the exchange rate.

# Getting **There**

### By Plane

Paris has two international airports. At **CHARLES DE GAULLE,** Air France flights arrive at Aerogate 2, while all other flights come into Aerogate 1. ☎ 01-48-62-22-80. At **ORLY,** international flights arrive at Orly Sud (South) and domestic flights at Orly Ouest (West). ☎ 01-49-75-15-15. Free **SHUTTLE BUSES** operate between the airports. Charles de Gaulle is larger and has more transport options into Paris.

**FROM CHARLES DE GAULLE: RER TRAINS** leave every 15 minutes between 5am and midnight, serving several of the major downtown Métro stations (trip time: 30 min.). Air France also operates two **SHUTTLE BUS** services into Paris, departing every 12 minutes (5:35am–11pm) for the place d'Etoile and porte Maillot, and every 30 minutes (7am–9:30pm) for the Gare Montparnesse and the Gare de Lyon. A **TAXI** to the city costs about 40€; the fare is higher at night (8pm–7am). The trip takes 40 to 50 minutes by bus or taxi.

**FROM ORLY:** There are no direct trains to central Paris, but the airport is served by **MONORAIL (ORLY VAL).** Change at the RER station Anthony for RER services into the city (trip time: about 30 min.). Air France **BUSES** leave from Orly Ouest and Orly Sud every 12 minutes (5:45am–11pm) for the Gare des Invalides, where you can catch a taxi or the Métro. A **TAXI** from the airport into Paris costs about 35€ (more at night). It takes 25 minutes to an hour to get to Paris by bus or taxi, depending on traffic.

### By Car

The main **HIGHWAYS** into Paris are the A-1 from the north (Great Britain and Benelux); A-13 from Rouen, Normandy, and northwest France; A-10 from Bordeaux, the Pyrenees, southwest France, and Spain; A-6 from Lyon, the French Alps, the Riviera, and Italy; and A-4 from eastern France.

### By Train

North Americans can buy a **EURAILPASS** or individual tickets from most travel agencies, or at any office of **RAIL EUROPE.** ☎ 877/272-RAIL; www.raileurope.com. From the U.K., you can travel to Paris under the English Channel via the **EUROSTAR EXPRESS** (trip time: about 3 hr.). Buy tickets directly from Eurostar. ☎ 800/EUROSTAR from the U.S., 0870/584-8848 in London, 01-55-31-54-54 in Paris; www.eurostar.com.

### By Bus

Bus travel to Paris is available from London and several other cities on the Continent. The arrival and departure point for Europe's largest bus operator, **EUROLINES FRANCE,** is a 35-minute Métro ride from central Paris, at the terminus of Métro line 3 (Galleini). Because Eurolines doesn't have sales agents outside Europe, most non-European travelers wait until they reach the Continent to buy their tickets. Any European travel agent can arrange this for you, or if you're in London you can go directly to **EUROLINES U.K.** 52 Grosvenor Gardens, Victoria, London SW1, ☎ 020/7730-8235; www.eurolines.co.uk.

# Getting **Around**

## By Public Transportation
Paris has one of the best public transport systems in the world. The **METRO** network is vast, reliable, and cheap, and within Paris you can transfer between the subway and the RER regional trains at no extra cost. The Métro runs from 5:30am to 1:15am daily, but the last train may pass through central Paris as much as an hour before that time. Also note that, while the Métro is reasonably safe at any hour, you should always use your common sense, and be on your guard for pickpockets. A bulk purchase of 10 tickets (called a *carnet*) costs 10€. If you don't need that many, you can buy single tickets. **BUSES** are reliable, but much slower than the Métro. Most buses run from 7am to 8:30pm, with only a few running at night. Services are limited on Sunday and public holidays. At certain stops, signs list the destinations and numbers of the buses serving that point. Bus and Métro fares are the same, and you can use the same carnets on both.

## By Taxi
You can hail a taxi when its sign reads LIBRE. The flag drops at 4.25€, and from 7am to 7pm you pay 1€ per kilometer, rising to 1.20€ the rest of the time. Cabs are scarce during rush hour. Unlicensed cabs (which are usually just a person with a car) may seem like a cheap alternative, but don't use them under any circumstances. You could find yourself the victim of a robbery—or worse. If you need to call a cab, try **LES TAXIS BLEUS.** ☎ *08-25-16-10-10.*

## By Car
Driving in Paris is not recommended for neophytes. Parking is difficult, traffic is dense, and networks of one-way streets make navigation, even with the best of maps, a problem. You would be much better advised to make use of the extensive public transport system, or to take cabs.

## By Foot
The best way to take in the city is to walk. The center is very pedestrian-friendly, and so long as you follow all the usual rules of thumb—buy a good map (or carry this guide with you), and stick to busy, well-lit places at night—you're bound to make a few unexpected discoveries along the way.

# Fast **Facts**

**APARTMENT RENTAL** A California-based company promoting upmarket B&B accommodations in Paris is **European B&B,** 437 J St., Suite 210, San Diego, CA 92101 (☎ **800/872-2632;** www.parisbandb.com). In Paris, contact their affiliate, **Alcôve & Agapes,** 8 bus rue Coysevox, 75018, Paris (☎ **01-44-85-06-05**).

**ATMS/CASHPOINTS** The easiest and best way to get cash abroad is through an ATM—the **Cirrus** and **PLUS** networks span the globe. Most banks charge a fee for international withdrawals—check with your bank before you leave home. **BABYSITTERS** The best selection of English-speaking sitters is found at **Kid Services** (☎ **08-20-00-02-30**).

**BANKS** Most banks are open Monday to Friday from 9am to 4:30pm. A few are open on Saturday. Shops and most hotels will cash traveler's checks, but not at the advantageous rate most banks and foreign exchanges will give you.

**BIKE RENTALS** **Paris-Vêlos,** 2 rue du Fer-à-Moulin, 5e (☎ **01-43-37-59-22;** Métro: Censier-Daubenton), rents bicycles by the day, weekend, or week. You must leave a 300€ deposit.

**BUSINESS HOURS** Shops tend to open from 9:30am to 5pm, but opening hours can be a little erratic. Some traditional shops open at 8am and close at 8 or 9pm, but the lunch break can last up to 3 hours, starting at 1pm. Most museums close 1 day a week (often Tues) and on national holidays.

**CONSULATES & EMBASSIES** **U.S. Embassy,** 2 av. Gabriel, 8e (☎ **01-43-12-47-08**); **U.S. Consulate,** 2 rue St-Florentin (☎ **01-43-12-22-22;** Métro: Concorde); **Canadian Embassy,** 35 av. Montaigne, 8e (☎ **01-44-43-29-00**); **U.K. Embassy,** 35 rue Faubourg St-Honoré, 8e (☎ **01-44-51-31-00**); **U.K. Consulate,** 18 bis rue d'Anjou, 8e (☎ **01-44-51-31-02**); **Irish Embassy,** 4 rue Rude, 16e (☎ **01-44-17-67-00**); **Australian Embassy,** 4 rue Jean-Ray, 15e (☎ **01-40-59-33-00**); **New Zealand Embassy,** 7 ter, rue Lêonard-de-Vinci, 16e (☎ **01-45-00-24-11**).

**CREDIT CARDS** Credit cards are a safe way to carry money. They also provide a convenient record of all your expenses, and they generally offer good exchange rates. You can also withdraw cash advances from your credit cards at banks or ATMs (cashpoints), provided you know your PIN. (Call the number on the back of your card if you don't know yours.) Keep in mind that when you use your credit card abroad, most banks assess a 2% fee above the 1% fee charged by Visa, MasterCard, or American Express.

**CURRENCY EXCHANGE** Cash your traveler's checks at banks or foreign exchange offices, not at shops or hotels. Most post offices change traveler's checks or convert money as well. Currency exchanges are also found at Paris airports and train stations, and along most of the major boulevards.

**CUSTOMS** **Non-E.U. nationals** can bring in, duty free, 200 cigarettes, 50 cigars, 2 liters of wine, and either 1 liter of alcohol over 22 proof, or 2 liters under 22 proof. Customs officials tend to be lenient about general merchandise, realizing the limits are unrealistically low. **E.U. citizens** can bring any amount of goods into France, so long as they are intended for personal use—not for resale.

**DENTISTS** See "Emergencies," below.

**DOCTORS** See "Emergencies," below.

**DRUGSTORES** After regular hours, ask at your hotel where the nearest 24-hour pharmacy is. You'll also find the address posted on the doors or windows of other drugstores in the neighborhood. One all-night drugstore is **Pharmacie Derhy,** in La Galerie Les Champs, 84 av. des Champs-Elysées, 8e (☎ **01-45-62-02-41**).

**EMERGENCIES** For the **police,** call ☎ 17. To report a **fire,** call ☎ 18. For an **ambulance,** call the fire department at ☎ **01-45-78-74-52;** or **S.A.M.U.,** a private ambulance company, at ☎ 15. From your cellphone, the emergency number is ☎ 112. If you need nonurgent medical attention, practitioners in most fields can be found at the **Centre Médical Europe,** 44 rue d'Amsterdam, 9e (☎ **01-42-81-93-33.**) For emergency dental service, call **S.O.S. Dentaire,** 87 bd. du Port-Royal, 13e (☎ **01-43-37-51-00**), Monday through Friday from 8pm to midnight, and Saturday and Sunday from 9:30am to midnight. **U.K. nationals** must have a completed and validated E111 form to receive full health benefits in France. The system for these recently changed. Starting in 2005, you need to apply for a new form. From January 1, 2006, visitors will need the European Health Insurance Card to receive free treatment. For advice, ask at your local post office or see www.dh.gov.uk/travellers.

**EVENT LISTINGS** *Pariscope* includes a listings section in English. Also available are *Officiel des Spectacles* and *Zurban*. *Le Figaro* carries a special listings supplement every Wednesday.

**FAMILY TRAVEL** The two official websites of the French Tourist Board, **France Tourism** (www.francetourism.com) and **France Guide** (www.franceguide.com), both have sections on family travel, the latter specifically aimed at kids. **Family Travel** (www.familytravel.com) is an independent, U.S.-based website offering reviews, sightseeing suggestions, and so on.

**GAY & LESBIAN TRAVELERS** **Ecoute Gay** (☎ 08-10-81-10-57) is a hot line offering counseling for persons with gay-related problems. **La Maison des Femmes** (☎ 01-43-43-41-13) offers information about Paris for lesbians. Paris's largest gay bookstore is **Les Mots à la Bouche**, 6 rue Ste.-Croix-de-la-Bretonnerie, 4th (☎ 01-42-78-88-30).

**HOLIDAYS** Public holidays include: New Year's Day (Jan 1); Easter Monday (Mar or Apr); Labor Day (May 1); Victory Day 1945 (May 8); Ascension Day (40 days after Easter); Whit Monday (11 days after Ascension Day); National Day/Bastille Day (July 14); Assumption Day (Aug 15); All Saints' Day (Nov 1); Armistice Day 1918 (Nov 11); and Christmas Day (Dec 25).

**INSURANCE** North Americans with homeowner's or renter's insurance are probably covered for lost luggage. If not, inquire with **Travel Assistance International** (☎ 800/821-2828) or **Travelex** (☎ 800/228-9792). These insurers can also provide trip-cancellation, medical, and emergency evacuation coverage abroad. The website www.moneysupermarket.com compares prices across a wide range of providers for single- and multi-trip policies. **For U.K. citizens,** insurance is always advisable, even if you have form E111. (See "Emergencies," above.)

**INTERNET ACCESS** Some of the more expensive hotels offer Internet access; alternatively, to surf the Net or check your e-mail, try **Rendezvous Toyota,** 79 av. des Champs-Elysées, 8e (☎ **01-56-89-29-79;** www.lerendezvoustoyota.com).

**LIQUOR LAWS** Supermarkets, grocery stores, and cafes sell alcoholic beverages. The legal drinking age is 16, but children under that age can be served alcohol in a bar or restaurant if accompanied by a parent or legal guardian. Hours of cafes vary; some even stay open 24 hours. It's illegal to drive while drunk. If convicted, motorists face a stiff fine and a possible prison term.

**LOST PROPERTY** If your luggage is lost, immediately file a lost-luggage claim at the airport, detailing the luggage contents. For most airlines, you must report delayed, damaged, or lost baggage within 4 hours of arrival.

**MAIL & POST OFFICES** Most post offices in Paris are open Monday through Friday from 8am to 7pm and Saturday from 8am to noon. However, the **main post office (PTT),** at 52 rue du Louvre (☎ **01-40-28-76-00**) is open 24 hours a day for stamps, phone calls, and sending faxes and telegrams. Stamps can usually be purchased from your hotel reception desk and at cafes with red TABAC signs.

**MONEY** The currency of France is the euro, which can be used in most other E.U. countries. The exchange rate varies, but at press time, 1€ was equal to $1.30 and £.70. The best way to get cash in Paris is at ATMs or cashpoints (see above). Credit cards are accepted at almost all shops, restaurants, and hotels, but you should always have some cash on hand for incidentals and sightseeing admissions.

**NEWSPAPERS & MAGAZINES** English-language newspapers are available from most kiosks, including the *International Herald Tribune* and *USA Today,* and British papers such as *The Times* and *The Independent.* The leading French-language domestic papers are *Le Monde, Le Figaro,* and *Libération.*

**PASSPORTS** If your passport is lost or stolen, contact your country's embassy or consulate immediately. (See "Consulates & Embassies," above.) Before you travel, you should copy the critical pages and keep them in a separate place.

**POLICE** Call ☎ 17 for emergencies. The principal *préfecture* (police station) is at 9 bd. du Palais, 4e (☎ **01-53-71-53-73;** Metro: Cité).

**SAFETY** Be especially aware of child pickpockets. Their method is to get very close to a target, ask for a handout, and deftly help themselves to your money or passport. Robbery at gun- or knifepoint is rare, but not unknown. For more information, consult the U.S. State Department's website at www. travel.state.gov; in the U.K., consult the Foreign Office's website, www. fco.gov.uk; and in Australia, consult the government travel advisory service at www.smartraveller. gov.au.

**SENIOR TRAVELERS** Mention that you're a senior when you make your travel reservations. As in most cities, people over the age of 60 qualify for reduced admission to theaters, museums, and other attractions, as well as discounted fares on public transport.

**SMOKING** Smoking is common in France, but authorities are clamping down heavily on smoking in public places, and it's now banned in such places as theaters and on public transport. Restaurants are obliged to provide nonsmoking areas, but they are often the worst tables available.

**TAXES** Value Added Tax, or VAT (TVA in French) is 19.6%, but non-E.U. visitors can get a refund if you spend 182€ or more in any store that participates in the VAT refund program. The shops will give you a form, which you must get stamped at Customs. (Allow extra time.) Mark the paperwork to request a credit card refund; otherwise you'll be stuck with a check in euros. An option is to ask for a **Global Refund form** (☎ 800/566-9828; www. globalrefund.com) when you make your purchase, and take it to a Global Refund counter at the airport. Your money is refunded on the spot, minus a commission.

**TELEPHONES** Public phones are found in cafes, Métro stations, and post offices, and occasionally on the street. Coin-operated telephones are rare. Most phones take *télécartes,* prepaid calling cards available at kiosks, post offices, and Métro stations. They cost 7.45€ or 15€ for 50 or 120 units, respectively. To make a **direct international call,** first dial 00, then dial the country code, the area code, and the local number. The country code for the **U.S.** and **Canada** is 1; **Great Britain,** 44; **Ireland,** 353; **Australia,** 61; and **New Zealand,** 64. You can also call the U.S., Canada, the U.K., Ireland, Australia, or New Zealand using **USA Direct/AT&T World Connect,** which allows you to avoid hotel surcharges. From **within France,** dial

☎ 0800/99-00-11-10-11, then follow the prompts.

**TICKETS** There are many theater ticket agencies in Paris, but buying tickets directly from the box office or at a discount agency can be up to 50% cheaper. Try **Kiosque Theâtre,** 15 place de la Madeleine (no phone). Tickets for many shows, events, and tours can also be purchased in advance in your home country through your travel agent or through **Keith Prowse** (☎ 800/233-6108 from the U.S., or 08701-23-24-25 from the U.K.; www.keithprowse.com).

**TIPPING** In cafes and restaurants, waiter service is usually included, though you can round the bill up or leave some small change, if you like. Tip taxi drivers 12% to 15%. Tip hotel porters 1€ to 1.50€ for each piece of luggage.

**TOILETS** If you use a toilet at a cafe or brasserie, it's customary to make some small purchase. In the street, the domed self-cleaning lavatories are a decent option if you have small change. Métro stations usually have public toilets, but the degree of cleanliness varies. Be prepared—in some places, the facilities on offer may be nothing more than a hole in the floor.

**TOURIST OFFICES** For tourist information, try **Espace du Tourisme,** Carrousel du Louvre, 99 rue de Rivoli (☎ 08-03-81-80-00 or 01-44-50-19-98); or **Office du Tourisme,** 127 av. des Champs-Elysées (☎ 01-49-52-53-54, or 01-49-52-53-56 for recorded information in English).

**TOURS** The two largest tour companies are **Globus/Cosmos** (☎ 800/338-7092; www.globusandcosmos.com) and **Trafalgar** (☎ 800/854-0103; www.trafalgartours.com). Many major airlines offer air/land package deals that include tours of Paris; ask the airlines or your travel agent for details.

**TRAVELERS WITH DISABILITIES** Nearly all modern hotels in France now have rooms designed for people with disabilities, but many older hotels do not. Most high-speed trains within France have wheelchair access, and guide dogs ride free. **Paris Info** (www.parisinfo.com) has resources for travelers with disabilities, including a list of accessible hotels. The **Association des Paralysés de France** (☎ 01-40-78-69-00; www.apf.asso.fr) provides help for individuals who use wheelchairs.

# Paris: **A Brief History**

**2000 B.C.** The Parisii tribe found the settlement of Lutétia alongside the Seine.

**52 B.C.** Julius Caesar conquers Lutétia during the Gallic Wars.

**300** Lutétia is renamed Paris; Roman power begins to weaken in France.

**1422** England invades Paris during the Hundred Years' War.

**1429** Joan of Arc tries to regain Paris for the French; she is later burned at the stake by the English in Rouen.

**1572** The Wars of Religion reach their climax with the St. Bartholomew's Day massacre of Protestants.

**1598** Henri IV endorses the Edict of Nantes, granting tolerance to Protestants.

**1643** Louis XIV moves his court to the newly built Versailles.

**1789** The French Revolution begins.

**1793** Louis XVI and his queen, Marie Antoinette, are publicly guillotined.

**1799** A coup d'état installs Napoleon Bonaparte as head of government.

**1804** Napoleon declares France an empire and is crowned emperor at Notre-Dame.

**1804–15** The Napoleonic wars.

**1814** Paris is briefly occupied by a coalition including Britain and Russia. The Bourbon monarchy is restored.

**1848** Revolutions across Europe; King Louis-Philippe is deposed by the autocratic Napoleon III.

**1860s** The Impressionist style of painting emerges.

**1870–71** The Franco-Prussian War ends in the siege of Paris. The Third Republic is established, while much of the city is controlled by the revolutionary Paris Commune.

**1914–18** World War I rips apart Europe. Millions killed in the trenches of northeast France.

**1940** German troops occupy France during World War II. The French Resistance under Gen. Charles de Gaulle maintains symbolic headquarters in London.

**1944** U.S. troops liberate Paris; de Gaulle returns in triumph.

**1958** France's Fourth Republic collapses; General de Gaulle is called out of retirement to head the Fifth Republic.

**1968** Parisian students and factory workers engage in a general revolt; the government is overhauled in the aftermath.

**1994** François Mitterrand and Queen Elizabeth II open the Channel Tunnel.

**1995** Jacques Chirac is elected president over François Mitterrand; Paris is crippled by a general strike.

**2002** The euro replaces the franc as France's national currency.

**2003–04** French opposition to the war in Iraq causes the largest diplomatic rift with the U.S. in decades.

# French **Architecture**

**This section serves as a guide** to some of the architectural styles you'll see in Paris. However, it's worth pointing out that very few buildings (especially churches) were built in one particular style. These massive, expensive structures often took centuries to complete, during which time tastes changed and plans were altered.

### Romanesque (800–1100)

Taking their inspiration from ancient Rome, the Romanesque architects concentrated on building large churches with wide aisles. Few examples of the Romanesque style remain in Paris, but the church of **St-Germain-des-Prés** (oldest part, 6th c. A.D.) is a good example. The overall building is Romanesque, but by the time builders got to creating the choir, the early Gothic was on— note the pointy arches.

## Gothic (1100–1500)

By the 12th century, engineering developments freed church architecture from the heavy, thick walls of Romanesque structures.

Instead of dark, somber, relatively unadorned Romanesque interiors that forced the eyes of the faithful toward the altar, the Gothic interior enticed the churchgoers' gaze upward to high ceilings filled with light. The squat, brooding Romanesque exteriors were replaced by graceful buttresses and spires. Arguably the finest example of Gothic church architecture anywhere in the world is **Notre-Dame** (1163–1250).

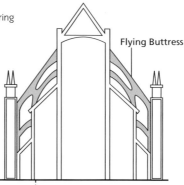

*Cross section of a Gothic church.*

Flying Buttress

## Renaissance (1500–1630)

In architecture, as in painting, the Renaissance came from Italy and took some time to coalesce. And, as in painting, its rules stressed proportion, order, classical inspiration, and precision, resulting in unified, balanced structures. The 1544 **Hôtel Carnavalet** (23 rue de Sévigné), a Renaissance mansion, is the only 16th-century hotel left in Paris. It contains the **Musée Carnavalet,** a museum devoted to the history of Paris and the French Revolution.

## Classicism & Rococo (1630–1800)

From the mid–17th century, France took the fundamentals of Renaissance classicism even further, finding inspiration in the classic era. During the reign of Louis XIV, art and architecture were subservient to political ends. Buildings were grandiose and severely ordered on the Versailles model. Opulence was saved for interior decoration, which increasingly became an excessively detailed and self-indulgent rococo (*rocaille* in French). Rococo tastes didn't last long, though, and soon a neoclassical movement was raising structures such as Paris's **Panthéon** (1758), based even more strictly on ancient models than the earlier classicism was.

## The 19th Century

Architectural styles in 19th-century Paris were eclectic, beginning in a severe classical mode and ending with something of an identity crisis—torn between Industrial Age technology and Art Nouveau organic. During the reign of Emperor Napoleon III (1852–70), classicism was reinterpreted in an ornate, dramatic mode. Urban planning was the architectural rage, and Paris became a city of wide boulevards courtesy of **Baron Georges-Eugène Haussmann** (1809–91), commissioned by Napoleon III in 1852 to redesign the city. Paris owes much of its remarkably unified look to Haussmann.

Expositions in 1878, 1889, and 1900 were the catalysts for constructing huge glass-and-steel structures that showed off modern techniques. This produced such Parisian monuments as the **Tour Eiffel** and **Sacré-Coeur.** However, the subsequent emergence of the Art Nouveau movement was, in many ways, a rebellion against such late-19th-century industrial zeal. Peaking around the turn of the century, it celebrated the unique nature of asymmetrical, curvaceous designs, often based on plants and flowers. It was during this short period that the famous Art Nouveau **Métro station**

**entrances** were designed by **Hector Guimard** (1867–1942). A recently renovated entrance is at the **porte Dauphine** station on the No. 2 line.

### The 20th Century

The ravages of war stalled the progress of French architecture for a number of decades, but the latter half of the 20th century was to see some the most audacious architectural projects in French history—and certainly some of the most controversial. Only gradually have structures such as the **Centre Pompidou** or the **Louvre**'s glass pyramids become accepted by most Parisians. Over time, perhaps they will become as beloved as the once-despised Tour Eiffel.

*La Tour Eiffel.*

# Useful Phrases & Menu Terms

**It's amazing how often a word or two of halting French** will change your hosts' disposition. At the very least, try to learn basic greetings, and—above all—the life-raft phrase, *Parlez-vous anglais?* ("Do you speak English?")

### Useful Words & Phrases

| ENGLISH | FRENCH | PRONUNCIATION |
|---|---|---|
| *Yes/No* | **Oui/Non** | wee/noh |
| *Okay* | **D'accord** | *dah*-core |
| *Please* | **S'il vous plaît** | seel voo *play* |
| *Thank you* | **Merci** | *mair*-see |
| *You're welcome* | **De rien** | duh ree-*ehn* |
| *Hello (during daylight)* | **Bonjour** | bohn-*jhoor* |
| *Good evening* | **Bonsoir** | bohn-*swahr* |
| *Goodbye* | **Au revoir** | o ruh-*vwahr* |
| *What's your name?* | **Comment vous appellez-vous?** | kuh-*mahn* voo za-pell-ay-*voo?* |
| *My name is* | **Je m'appelle** | *jhuh* ma-pell |
| *How are you?* | **Comment allez-vous?** | kuh-*mahn* tahl-ay-*voo?* |

| ENGLISH | FRENCH | PRONUNCIATION |
|---|---|---|
| So-so | Comme ci, comme ça | kum-see, kum-sah |
| I'm sorry/Excuse me | Pardon | pahr-dohn |
| Do you speak English? | Parlez-vous anglais? | par-lay-voo zahn-glay? |
| I don't speak French | Je ne parle pas français | jhuh ne parl pah frahn-say |
| I don't understand | Je ne comprends pas | jhuh ne kohm-prahn pas |
| Where is . . . ? | Où est . . . ? | ooh eh . . . ? |
| Why? | Pourquoi? | poor-kwah? |
| here/there | ici/là | ee-see/lah |
| left/right | à gauche/à droite | a goash/a drwaht |
| straight ahead | tout droit | too drwah |
| I want to get off at . . . | Je voudrais descendre à . . . | jhe voo-dray day-son-drah ah . . . |
| airport | l'aéroport | lair-o-por |
| bridge | pont | pohn |
| bus station | la gare routière | lah gar roo-tee-air |
| bus stop | l'arrêt de bus | lah-ray duh boohss |
| cathedral | cathedral | ka-tay-dral |
| church | église | ay-gleez |
| hospital | l'hôpital | low-pee-tahl |
| museum | le musée | luh mew-zay |
| police | la police | lah po-lees |
| one-way ticket | aller simple | ah-lay sam-pluh |
| round-trip ticket | aller-retour | ah-lay re-toor |
| ticket | un billet | uh bee-yay |
| toilets | les toilettes/les WC | lay twa-lets/les vay-say |

## In Your Hotel

| ENGLISH | FRENCH | PRONUNCIATION |
|---|---|---|
| bathtub | une baignoire | ewn bayn-nwar |
| hot and cold water | l'eau chaude et froide | low showed ay fwad |
| Is breakfast included? | Petit déjeuner inclus? | peh-tee day-jheun-ay ehn-klu? |
| room | une chambre | ewn shawm-bruh |
| shower | une douche | ewn dooch |
| sink | un lavabo | uh la-va-bow |

## The Calendar

| ENGLISH | FRENCH | PRONUNCIATION |
|---|---|---|
| Sunday | dimanche | dee-mahnsh |
| Monday | lundi | luhn-dee |
| Tuesday | mardi | mahr-dee |
| Wednesday | mercredi | mair-kruh-dee |
| Thursday | jeudi | jheu-dee |
| Friday | vendredi | vawn-druh-dee |
| Saturday | samedi | sahm-dee |
| yesterday | hier | ee-air |
| today | aujourd'hui | o-jhord-dwee |
| this morning/this afternoon | ce matin/cet après-midi | suh ma-tan/set ah-preh mee-dee |

| ENGLISH | FRENCH | PRONUNCIATION |
|---------|--------|---------------|
| *tonight* | ce soir | suh *swahr* |
| *tomorrow* | demain | de-*man* |

## Food, Menu & Cooking Terms

| ENGLISH | FRENCH | PRONUNCIATION |
|---------|--------|---------------|
| *I would like* | Je voudrais | jhe voo-*dray* |
| *to eat* | manger | mahn-*jhay* |
| *Please give me* | Donnez-moi, s'il vous plaît | doe-nay-*mwah*, seel voo play |
| *a bottle of* | une bouteille de | ewn boo-*tay* duh |
| *a cup of* | une tasse de | ewn tass duh |
| *a glass of* | un verre de | uh vair duh |
| *a cocktail* | un apéritif | uh ah-pay-ree-*teef* |
| *the check/bill* | l'addition/la note | la-dee-see-*ohn*/ la noat |
| *a knife* | un couteau | uh koo-*toe* |
| *a napkin* | une serviette | ewn sair-vee-*et* |
| *a spoon* | une cuillère | ewn kwee-*air* |
| *a fork* | une fourchette | ewn four-*shet* |
| *fixed-price menu* | un menu | uh may-*new* |
| *Is the tip/service included?* | Est-ce que le service est compris? | ess-ke luh ser-*vees* eh com-*pree?* |
| *Waiter!/Waitress!* | Monsieur!/ Mademoiselle! | mun-*syuh*/mad-mwa-*zel* |
| *wine list* | une carte des vins | ewn cart day *van* |
| *appetizer* | une entrée | ewn en-*tray* |
| *main course* | un plat principal | uh plah pran-see-*pahl* |
| *tip included* | service compris | sehr-*vees* cohm-*pree* |
| *tasting/chef's menu* | menu dégustation | may-*new* day-gus-ta-see-*on* |

## Numbers

| ENGLISH | FRENCH | PRONUNCIATION |
|---------|--------|---------------|
| *0* | zéro | *zeh*-roh |
| *1* | un | uhn |
| *2* | deux | duh |
| *3* | trois | twah |
| *4* | quatre | *kah*-truh |
| *5* | cinq | sank |
| *6* | six | seess |
| *7* | sept | set |
| *8* | huit | weet |
| *9* | neuf | nuhf |
| *10* | dix | deess |
| *11* | onze | ohnz |
| *12* | douze | dooz |
| *13* | treize | trehz |
| *14* | quatorze | kah-*torz* |
| *15* | quinze | kanz |
| *16* | seize | sez |

| ENGLISH | FRENCH | PRONUNCIATION |
|---------|--------|---------------|
| 17 | dix-sept | deez-set |
| 18 | dix-huit | deez-weet |
| 19 | dix-neuf | deez-noof |
| 20 | vingt | vehn |
| 30 | trente | trahnt |
| 40 | quarante | kah-rahnt |
| 50 | cinquante | sang-kahnt |
| 100 | cent | sahn |
| 1,000 | mille | meel |

# Toll-Free Numbers & Websites

**AER LINGUS**
☎ 800/474-7424 in the U.S.
☎ 01/886-8844 in Ireland
www.aerlingus.com

**AIR CANADA**
☎ 888/247-2262
www.aircanada.ca

**AIR FRANCE**
☎ 800/237-2747 in the U.S.
☎ 0820-820-820 in France
www.airfrance.com

**AIR NEW ZEALAND**
☎ 800/262-1234 or -2468 in the U.S.
☎ 800/663-5494 in Canada
☎ 0800/737-000 in New Zealand
www.airnewzealand.com

**ALITALIA**
☎ 800/223-5730 in the U.S.
☎ 8488-65641 in Italy
www.alitalia.it

**AMERICAN AIRLINES**
☎ 800/433-7300
www.aa.com

**AUSTRIAN AIRLINES**
☎ 800/843-0002 in the U.S.
☎ 43/(0)5-1789 in Austria
www.aua.com

**BMI**
No U.S. number
☎ 0870/6070-222 in Britain
www.flybmi.com

**BRITISH AIRWAYS**
☎ 800/247-9297 in the U.S.
☎ 0870/850-9-850 in Britain
www.british-airways.com

**CONTINENTAL AIRLINES**
☎ 800/525-0280
www.continental.com

**DELTA AIR LINES**
☎ 800/221-1212
www.delta.com

**EASYJET**
No U.S. number
www.easyjet.com

**IBERIA**
☎ 800/772-4642 in the U.S.
☎ 902/400-500 in Spain
www.iberia.com

**ICELANDAIR**
☎ 800/223-5500 in the U.S.
☎ 354/50-50-100 in Iceland
www.icelandair.is

**KLM**
☎ 800/374-7747 in the U.S.
☎ 020/4 747 747 in the Netherlands
www.klm.nl

**LUFTHANSA**
☎ 800/645-3880 in the U.S.
☎ 49//(0)-180-5-838426 in Germany
www.lufthansa.com

**NORTHWEST AIRLINES**
☎ 800/225-2525
www.nwa.com

**QANTAS**
☎ 800/227-4500 in the U.S.
☎ 612/131313 in Australia
www.qantas.com

**SCANDINAVIAN AIRLINES**
☎ 800/221-2350 in the U.S.
☎ 0070/727-727 in Sweden
☎ 70/10-20-00 in Denmark

☎ 358/(0)20-386-000 in Finland
☎ 815/200-400 in Norway
www.scandinavian.net

**SWISS INTERNATIONAL AIRLINES**
☎ 877/359-7947 in the U.S.
☎ 0848/85-2000 in Switzerland
www.swiss.com

**UNITED AIRLINES**
☎ 800/241-6522
www.united.com

**US AIRWAYS**
☎ 800/428-4322
www.usairways.com

**VIRGIN ATLANTIC AIRWAYS**
☎ 800/862-8621 in continental U.S.
☎ 0870/380-2007 in Britain
www.virgin-atlantic.com

# Index

# Photo **Credits**